Downstairs
the Queen
is Knitting

ALSO BY DORCAS SMUCKER,

Upstairs the Peasants are Revolting

Ordinary Days

Downstairs the Queen is Knitting

DORCAS SMUCKER

Good Books
New York, New York

Credits
All the essays in this book were first published in the *The Register-Guard*, Eugene, Oregon, except for "Apple Dumplings," which first appeared in *The Simple Home Almanac*, an online magazine produced by Peggy Hostetler.

The scripture references on pages 39, 82, 107, 109, and 119 are taken from the Holy Bible, King James Version.

The scripture reference on page 74 is taken from the Holy Bible, New International Version® NIV®. Copyright © 1973, 1978, 1984 by the International Bible Society. Used by permission of Zondervan. All rights reserved.

The publisher has made every effort, without success, to contact the prisoner for permission to reprint his letter and prayer-poem which appear on pages 15 and 16.

The photo on page 168 is by Amy Smucker. The photo on the back cover is by Ruth Swartzendruber.

Good Books books may be purchased in bulk at special discounts for sales promotion, corporate gifts, fund-raising, or educational purposes. Special editions can also be created to specifications. For details, contact the Special Sales Department, Good Books, 307 West 36th Street, 11th Floor, New York, NY 10018 or info@skyhorsepublishing.com.

Good Books is an imprint of Skyhorse Publishing, Inc.®, a Delaware corporation.

Visit our website at www.goodbooks.com.

10 9 8 7 6 5 4 3 2

Library of Congress Cataloging-in-Publication Data
Smucker, Dorcas.
Downstairs the queen is knitting / Dorcas Smucker.
    p. cm.
  ISBN 978-1-56148-667-0 (pbk. : alk. paper) 1. Country life--Oregon--Willamette River Valley--Anecdotes. 2. Farm life--Oregon--Willamette River Valley--Anecdotes. 3. Smucker, Dorcas--Family--Anecdotes. 4. Willamette River Valley (Or.)--Social life and customs--Anecdotes. 5. Willamette River Valley (Or.)--Biography--Anecdotes. 6. Mennonites--Oregon--Willamette River Valley--Biography--Anecdotes. 7. Spouses of clergy--Oregon--Willamette River Valley--Biography--Anecdotes. I. Title.
  F882.W6S54 2009
  306.87409795'3--dc22   2009008219

Cover art and design by Wendell Minor

Printed in the United States of America

To Matt, my firstborn —
You survived my first, frightened attempt at mothering.
We both survived your attempts to reconstruct the universe.
You will go far, and I am proud of you.

Table of Contents

Introduction

*R*aising a family is like a canoe trip down the Willamette River. You have a pretty good idea of where you want to go and how you want to get there, but the actual journey involves things you weren't expecting: a swift current, dangerous snags, swirling eddies, and lots of seemingly unproductive hard work, as well as the unexpected beauty of leafy sunshine on the water and determined ospreys diving for fish.

This book is a collection of essays about rural life in Oregon's Willamette Valley. It's about the strange, surprising journey of family life, about joy and laughter as well as guilt and grace and grief. It's about legacies and children and travels and marriage and loss.

These stories revolve around my husband and me and our six children. Written over a three-year period, they do not appear in chronological order, so you can open the book at random and peruse a chapter of your choice. Each one, I am told, is as long as a cup of coffee. Some are sweet, some black, some with lots of cream.

Growing Up

Silly Putty on the Quilt: This, Too, Shall Pass

*L*ife is never dull with two preteen boys.

Steven is 11, Ben is 12, and all day, the action never seems to stop. They eat mountains of calories and beg for more the instant the dishes are done. They spring into the air and slap their grimy hands on the door frames every time they walk through. Everything not nailed down, such as eggs or quart jars of green beans, must be tossed into the air and (usually) caught, every napping person wakened, every phone conversation disrupted.

They hold burping contests and comb-and-paper kazoo concerts and karate-chopping-cookies demonstrations. They put rocks in each other's ears, whack each other with canoe paddles, and soak each other when they're supposed to be washing the van. They break their little sister's hoe—accidentally, they insist—and my favorite china saucer. They feed ice cream to the cat, leave their sandals in the yard for the dog to chew on, and try to hatch tadpoles in quart jars of slimy green water. They put a loaf of bread in the freezer, as instructed, then absentmindedly place a three-pound package of sausage on top of it.

Personal hygiene is a foreign concept. The boys would wear the same T-shirts every day until they stood stiffly at attention under their own power.

With Ben's digital camera, they make jittery movies with scenes that plunge sideways and swirl nauseatingly. One boy sweeps to the basket and dunks the ball while the other

7

holds the camera and hollers a commentary, trying to sound like Jerry Allen, the Ducks' announcer. Then they huddle their sweaty bodies in front of the computer and replay each scene backward and forward at high speeds, howling with laughter and shoving each other.

Mothering these boys is an exhausting job, complicated by the fact that I also have three older children and a 7-year-old daughter who thinks too much and never stops talking. "I wonder what I should do," she says, soaking in the bathtub, "if I'm all grown up and there's this guy who really likes me and he wants to marry me, but I don't really like him. What should I do, Mom? I mean, he might be nice and stuff. And I'd feel sorry for him. But if I don't like him I don't want to marry him, you know?"

One day I decided I deserved a break and sat down to eat a slice of pie and read one section of the newspaper. What are the chances, I wondered, that I can get through this pie and this paper without being interrupted? Zero, it turned out. I was interrupted 11 times—twice by the phone ringing, once by someone at the door, and eight times by children who "desperately" needed me.

I spend much of my time averting disaster and dealing with crises, always with the sense that I am forgetting something important and if I only had a moment to catch my breath I would remember what it was. What I need most and seldom get in this stage is perspective, a "this-too-shall-pass" mentality to give me a sense of humor and a wider view than today's broken eggs on the kitchen floor.

The truth, which I normally am too distracted to recognize, is that I have the perspective I need right under my nose. Matt, who is 20, and Amy, 18, are seldom around and make far less noise than their siblings, so I don't notice them as much. They spent hours in their rooms studying until finals week was over, and now they zip through the kitchen, grabbing an orange, on their way to work. Both of them are responsible young adults who take out the trash or clean bathrooms without complaining and call me on the way home to ask if I need milk or fresh fruit. Now and then, my husband and I sit up late with them and have long, refreshing discussions.

And both Matt and Amy, now that I think of it, used to be 12.

I was cleaning the attic recently when I found a stash of books and magazines: *Animals of North America*, *Encyclopedia of Animal Life*, *Reptile Digest*. It seemed like only yesterday when I had put them in the attic, and only the day before when they were all over Matt's room and he was consumed with his interest in animals.

I called Matt up to the attic and asked him what I should do with all these books. He looked them over, maneuvered his tall body down the attic ladder, and said casually, "You can give them all to Goodwill."

I wanted to cry. Suddenly I was nostalgic, actually sentimental, for the days when he was 10 or 12, spouting animal facts, arguing incessantly, losing his temper, and placing a jar of meat and flies on his windowsill and watching the entire biomass change into a seething pile of maggots.

Matt, who used to act like he would die if he had to dry dishes, was my lifesaver last week when we threw a surprise party for Amy's 18th birthday at a park in Peoria. He muscled tables, chairs, slow cookers, and pitchers into the cars and then helped me unload them all at the other end and reload them when the party was over. When did he turn into a considerate, helpful young man? I have no idea.

A few days after her party, Amy curled up on the couch with Paul and me for one of those precious late-night talks. "The other day I found my diary of when I was 12," she said. "You guys must have been really worried about me. 'I hate Dad!'" she quoted, laughing. "'He's just so harsh and domineering. I just hate it when he always lectures me. And Mom gets in bad moods and gets mad at people for nothing.'"

Amy was right: We were worried about her back then. She didn't like us, and I feared she never would. "Everything I say to her is the wrong thing," I wailed on the phone to my brother, who had a daughter the same age. I felt that we were losing Amy and I had no idea how to bring her back.

My brother, as I recall, tried to tell me that I was doing the important things right, everything would be OK, and Amy would not always be 12. I didn't believe him. Lost in the thunderstorms of that time, I saw no signs of the sunshine on this side or a laughing young woman sitting up late for a cozy talk with her mom and dad.

At Amy's party, I sat at a picnic table beside my sister-in-law, Rosie. "How are your kids doing?" she asked, genuinely interested as always.

"My big kids are turning into these really nice people," I said. "I'm so impressed with them."

"You sound surprised," Rosie said, amused.

"I never felt like I knew what I was doing as a mom," I told her. "I was always surprised when my children turned a year old because they had actually survived babyhood under my care. And when they turn into good adult people, I can hardly believe it, either."

Today, Steven's denim quilt showed up in the laundry hamper smeared with huge splotches of green Silly Putty. I have no idea how to clean it.

I see that, in spite of my careful instruction, all five of Ben's dresser drawers are open, all at different angles, with tired socks and shirts hanging over the edges and spilling onto the floor.

"This, too, shall pass," I tell myself. "Someday they'll grow up; someday you'll be surprised. Take a deep breath. Stay calm. Believe."

Gifts from a Child

Right on time on a Monday afternoon, my son Steven and I enter the small sanctuary at Emerald Baptist Church. His wet shoes squeak on the wood floor as he finds his seat in the third row. I sit toward the back and wait.

More boys come in, sniffing and cold, with raindrops in their hair. They shuck coats and toss them to their mothers, then bang on the piano, tap the drums, or clamber over the seats.

Tama, the director, takes her place and claps her hands: clap, clap, clapclapclap. The boys repeat the rhythm. Stragglers find their seats. Talkers quiet down. Tama slaps another short series. The boys repeat it.

Then the pianist plays a few notes and the weekly miracle happens as two dozen elbowing, noisy boys suddenly transform, with a burst of clear and beautiful song, into the Junior Boys' division of the Oregon Children's Choir. "Glo-o-o-o-ria," they sing, "Hosanna in excelsis!"

As the music swirls around me, I feel, as always, a mix of love and pride and vindication and awe and strange unnamed emotions. What gifts—this son, his talents, and the blessings he has given our family.

The Christmas story is about God choosing the most unlikely to bring the greatest gifts: a small child, poor and powerless, bringing redemption and hope to the world. God still works in children today, I believe, not in the cosmic sense of bringing salvation as Jesus did, but in subtle and gentle influences that we never thought to ask for.

Steven came home to us from Kenya two years ago on Christmas Eve, a small, shy, tired 10-year-old with a shaved head. It was soon obvious that Steven loved music. He could hear a tune once and whistle it perfectly. Everything became a song: On school mornings, he hopped to the bathroom after breakfast chanting "Teeth, face, hair!" to the tune of "Hot Cross Buns."

"You should develop his talent," my musical sister-in-law said. I took her word for it, since my husband, Paul, and I are not especially musical.

After much searching I found the Oregon Children's Choir and took Steven in for an audition last summer. He scored five-out-of-five on all the little exercises, and the director said she would be delighted to have him in the choir. It was a confirmation, again, of a divine touch on Steven's life—a former street orphan transformed into a loyal member of a children's choir in Oregon.

Today, Steven is six inches taller, 30 pounds heavier, and many times more noisy and active than when he first came. He has a nice crop of hair that clumps when he forgets to brush it.

Despite his arrival on Christmas Eve, Steven does not wear a halo. He fudges the truth at times, absentmindedly leaves scissors in the refrigerator, and is known as one of the Burp Kings at his school. Yet this does not disqualify him from blessing others, both in our immediate family and far beyond it, a comfort to those of us who sometimes wonder if we are too imperfect for God to use in his purposes on Earth.

One of Steven's many gifts to me comes when he sings. I thought I was at peace with my lack of music ability, yet something blissful and healing takes place when I watch

Steven singing in the choir, tall and confident in the back row. I finally feel compensated for a lifetime of failing choir tryouts, having the teacher tell me in front of everyone that I was singing too low, and not knowing how to sing the "shaped" do-mi-sol notes.

Steven has blessed our family in other ways as well.

"Have you noticed that Ben doesn't say 'I'm bored' anymore?" my daughter asked the other day.

She's right. Ben, who is 13, used to flop on the couch and complain that there was nothing to do. Not anymore. Now he has a willing buddy to toss a football with him, canoe down the creek, or practice burping.

Also, I had a troubling sense, a few years ago, that my husband's busyness was calling his heart and priorities away from his family. He traveled a lot and took on enormous amounts of work. When Steven came, Paul quit traveling and made sure he was at home every evening for six months to put Steven and the other children to bed. Paul chose this primarily for Steven's benefit, but I feel that it brought him back to the rest of us as well, and I am grateful.

Perhaps the most remarkable story of Steven's influence involved an inmate at a state prison in Salem. Every year our church helps with a project that delivers thousands of handmade Christmas cards, along with cookies and a small gift, to inmates in various prisons around the state. The schoolchildren help with this as well, coloring and signing dozens of cards.

Some time after last year's project, the director received a letter from a 21-year-old prisoner and read it at church. The young man wrote that one morning, discouraged and depressed, he tried to write a prayer in poetry form, but quit and threw it away. Later that day, he received the Christmas packet from our church. He ate the cookies and opened the card.

Then he wrote, "It made me cry. It said, 'Have a happy time. From Steven, age 10.' "Something hit me and I don't really know what…. It made me feel like there's somebody out there that really does care. I know he didn't know who was going to get it, but I believe with all my heart it was meant for me. Is it coincidence that I started with writing a prayer to God that day which I've never done, gave up, then received a card … from a little boy that opened my eyes and heart into something I can't explain?

"I would like you to know I feel weird writing all this. I'm supposed to be a tough guy and I'm still in a gang. But you know, I want help, I want to learn a different way of life.

"I ended up picking that poem out of the trash and I finished it. It's my first prayer to God and I owe it to that boy named Steven (who) by a simple card gave me something I've never ever had, a hope for a better way of life."

The prisoner's poem followed:

My First Prayer: Is There an Angel for Me?
(Dedicated to Steven, age 10)

Is there an extra angel, Lord
That maybe you could lend to me
I know this is a lot I'm asking for
While down on bended knee.
I've caused my world to crumble to pieces
I even pushed my family away
Coming up with excuses I called reasons

> Yet still I feel this pain
> With my hands to my face I close this prayer
> God please forgive me for all my sins
> Please show my family love and care
> Help lead me away from this life I live.
> Amen.

At this year's Festival of Trees, Steven stood with the other choristers, all handsome in their navy blue shirts and khaki pants, and sang: "Do you hear what I hear? Do you know what I know? A child, a child, he will bring us goodness and light."

Listening, I thought, "Yes, he does. Both that child and this one. Yes, I hear, I know."

The Blackberries of Parenting

I have lofty goals for my children. I expect them to grow up equipped with both wisdom and common sense, able to sense and avoid danger, ready to see a need and meet it, and eager to make a difference in the world. However, I have two adolescent boys who are not as enthusiastic about my goals and standards as I am. In fact, their ideas and mine seem to clash on a regular basis. This results not in me lowering my standards, but rather in plunging into despair because I'm sure I have failed as a mom.

A typical example of this is the recent event we now refer to as the Blackberry Episode. Wild blackberries are both a pest and a blessing in this part of the Willamette Valley. Uncontrolled, they take over any vacant area, smothering old machinery and small buildings and anything else in their way. But late every summer, along fence rows and behind old barns, they produce a crop of delicious berries, nestled among millions of vicious thorns, free to anyone brave enough to pick them.

I have found this a good enterprise for Ben, age 14, and Steven, 12, who like to attempt courageous feats and go exploring in jeans and rubber boots. As August turned into September, I sent them out every few days. They always returned with an ice cream bucket or two of berries, which I turned into pies, cobblers, and jars of pie filling for this winter. Their best picking spot was about half a mile away, across the neighbor's fescue field, along the railroad tracks.

One day I realized the rain would be coming soon and the blackberry season was about to end, so after supper I sent the boys on one last expedition, letting them out of doing dishes as a bonus. An hour or so later they came back, but with only part of a bucket of berries. Suspiciously, I demanded an explanation and Ben slowly complied. "Uh, well, you see, it's like this. We picked a full bucket of berries, plus about a third, and then we climbed the fence back into the field and headed home and I was like, 'Hey! Big wide-open field—let's see if we can walk 200 steps with our eyes closed!'"

I thought, "No no no. Please, no."

Steven traversed his 200 steps safely, I was told, and opened his eyes to see that Ben had veered off north toward Substation Drive and a fence. He yelled, but Ben ignored him, figuring Steven had stepped in a hole or something. Shortly after, at step 181, Ben crashed into the fence and spilled his entire bucket of berries irretrievably into the dirt and straw.

"Yeah."

I am not often at a loss for words, but when I heard this woeful tale I opened my mouth to say something, then shut it, shook my head, then opened my mouth again, then shut it again. The boys quickly leaped into the gap and said all the proper things such as, "We know it was really stupid; we're sorry; we'll never try that again; we'll pick more berries tomorrow."

My husband, Paul, then joined the conversation. "See, what you have to do is look around and make sure there's no fence within 200 steps in any direction before you try that."

My silent tongue let loose at this point in a shrill, "What? That's not the point! The point is that you think about the cargo in your hands before you do something that stupid! And you don't walk with your eyes shut with a bucket of blackberries in your hands, fence or no fence!"

Paul and the boys looked at me sympathetically, no doubt thinking, "Poor Mom, off on one of her rants again."

As always, I read far too much into the incident. I was failing as a mom; there was no doubt about that. All these years and I hadn't taught Ben and Steven a shred of common sense. If they lived to grow up they would no doubt someday try to walk 200 steps across a fescue field—or a busy highway—with their eyes closed, only with their first child in their arms rather than a bucket of berries.

Paul, in contrast, was calm and straightforward as always. "Well," he told me, "that's one of the disadvantages of having creative kids." He did not say out loud, but implied, "And I recall you were the one that always wanted creative kids."

My friend, Arlene, when I called her, was far more consoling. "Your boys are nice," she told me gently. "And they're smart, and they really are going to grow up into good people."

Parenting, I have decided, is much like a jaunt to the berry patch, best undertaken with courage and resolve and tall boots. You hope for a bucket of ripe berries in the end, but there are no guarantees. The thorns may be frustrating and sometimes even overwhelming, but the real challenge for me at this stage is to focus on the berries instead of the scratches I get in the process.

Despite the stupidity of the Blackberry Episode, I have to admit that overall, Arlene is right, and my boys are turning into nice people. For example, both Ben and Steven, for all their irritation at 8-year-old Jenny, will make her a peanut butter sandwich before they make their own. They take her swimming in the creek and exploring in ditches and woods. The other day, Steven actually emptied the kitchen garbage without being told. Ben gets himself up early to finish his homework. Both boys are kind to cats—one of the best indicators, in my experience, of a man's character. And the day after the Blackberry Episode, they headed across the fescue field without being told and returned with a full bucket of berries.

Sometimes, I've found, you push aside a large leaf among a thousand irritating thorns and find an unusually generous cluster of berries. Such was a little conversation I overheard recently, proof that despite my exasperation with them, the boys are absorbing the most important message of all—how truly loved they really are. Paul was on the couch one morning, reading that week's Sunday school lesson, a study from the book of Genesis about Isaac and Rebekah and how they each favored one of their twin sons, Jacob and Esau.

"Hey, Ben," I heard Paul saying, "Who's your mom's favorite child?" And Ben promptly replied with the perfect but completely unscripted answer: "It's a six-way tie for first place." As always, I read far too much into this, thinking tearfully, "OK, I can officially die happy now—I have succeeded as a mom after all."

Parenting, like picking blackberries, is a journey into perilous territory. Sticky refrigerator doors and spilled buckets and senseless arguments poke and irritate. But eventually, biting into the sweet steaming goodness of a slice of blackberry pie, the scratches and scars become worthwhile and almost forgotten.

The Mystery of Family

An episode seven years ago has found its way into our family lore, retold whenever someone is exasperatingly literal.

Jenny was a baby back then, going on 1 year old. I needed to put a hem in a jumper before we went away for the evening, so I plopped Jenny on the floor and asked 13-year-old Matt to keep her entertained for a few minutes. Then I turned to my sewing machine and hurriedly hemmed.

A few minutes later I heard a thud and Jenny started crying. "What happened?" I asked without turning around.

Matt said, "She fell over and bumped her head."

"Well, do something," I said distractedly. "Rub it where she bumped it or something."

Jenny kept crying. I turned around and couldn't comprehend, at first, what I was seeing. Jenny sat wailing forlornly on the floor while Matt, on his knees, had his hand on the edge of my sewing-supplies cabinet and was earnestly stroking it.

"Matthew Smucker, what on Earth are you doing?"

"You *said*, 'Rub it where she bumped it.'"

Not long ago, another of my children had what we now refer to as a Rub-It-Where-She-Bumped-It moment. I was making a huge batch of mashed potatoes, some for supper and the rest for a hot meal at our church school the next day. On the counter, raw sliced potatoes waited in a large pot while I finished mashing some cooked potatoes in the mixing bowl beside it.

Rushing around the kitchen, I handed 12-year-old Steven a large bowl and spoon and pointed toward the counter. "You dish up the potatoes for supper," I instructed. I cut the meat, stirred the vegetables, and turned to get the potatoes. Steven stood there, conscientiously piling chunks of raw potato into a tall heap in the serving bowl.

Once again there was a dumbfounded exclamation from me and a defensive, "But you *said* ..."

Around the table, I once more related the story of Matt "rubbing it where she bumped it," and both Matt and Steven were able to laugh at themselves.

I am endlessly intrigued with the dynamics of family, especially the differences and similarities between siblings. It is understandable that two brothers would both display such unbelievably narrow literalness, but the twist in this plot is that Matt was born to us and Steven was adopted. Steven's skin and hair are much darker than his redheaded siblings', but in matters of personality he is no more alike or different than the other five are to one other. The experts I read on the subject agree that two siblings can be very similar or they can be far more different in temperament and behavior than two people chosen at random.

I find, in our family, the strangest combinations and contrasts: Two brothers with very different personalities have the same heavy tread walking through the kitchen. Three of my children tend to take me seriously when I say something; to the other three, words from Mom are mere fluff in the wind, to be ignored unless something actually happens. The statistically unusual combination of reddish hair and brown eyes showed up in three of the children. The most prolific writer of the bunch had the hardest time learning to read.

The question, for me, is *why* they are the way they are. One would think offspring of one set of parents, raised in the same household, would be more predictably alike. The experts are no help here, droning on about nature vs. nurture, as though the only choices were A and B.

My own theory leans toward a third option, a mysterious force at work that goes far beyond genetics and environment. I think God handpicks children for the families they belong to, for reasons we may never understand. My friends, especially the adoptive moms, agree. "Steven is a true Smucker," they chuckle, referring to the independent, argumentative spirit common to all of my six. I see that trait as a gift: For all our variation, we have a common thread to identify us as a family, a reminder that we will always belong.

Sometimes, siblings seem to be designed to clash in order for them to learn to get along with anyone they'll encounter in the future. My two older daughters have always been so different that I wondered how they could come from the same set of parents. Amy is short and freckled and logical; Emily is tall and dark and dramatic. When they were little, we grew so tired of their fights that my husband once laid a broom down the center of their bed to delineate the two sides. I was horrified, the next morning, to discover this bunch of dirty bristles sticking out of the covers between their sleeping heads.

But somehow, over the years, their rough edges have polished each other and now they are the best of friends. They talk in an abbreviated code that I can't understand. As Emily recently wrote on her Xanga site, "Sisters, I think, have a certain ability to talk to each other using minimum words, and still understand each other perfectly. Amy and I, at least, have this ability. I wish Mom did, but she doesn't." And Amy wrote on her blog, "I love spending time with my sister. She is the most interesting person I know."

In other ways, I see my children with little quirks so similar it takes my breath away. Jenny, born almost 11 years after Amy and with the same red-gold hair and brown eyes, looks and acts so much like her big sister that I often feel like I'm reliving Amy's childhood. Winding up to read me a story that she wrote, Jenny hitches her shoulders back and takes a deep breath, precisely like Amy used to long before Jenny was born. How does this work? I wonder, watching. And why?

I believe God chose the eight of us for each other and did a much better job than if I had filled out the order forms myself. For all my annoyance when two siblings clash or a distracted child again "rubs it where she bumped it," I believe there is something mystical and miraculous going on here, and I am awed.

The Passing Summer of our Lives

J have neither scripture nor science to back me up on this, but I think summer in the Willamette Valley is about as close to heaven as we get here on Earth.

The days begin with sunshine burrowing through the oak trees along Muddy Creek and the curtains by my bed. They continue with the daily predictable combination of warm sun and low humidity, and end with the mountains turning a dusty '90s-decor blue as the sun sets behind Mary's Peak and the clouds hover like thick gold-edged ripples of quilt batting. The dry heat of midday cools to bearable every evening while we finish the supper dishes. Then I get on my bike and wander down Substation or Powerline roads, watching summer progress in the ditches and fields.

Huge flat fields change from green to a rich tan as the tall grass becomes piled windrows, cut and drying in the sun. Then they are harvested with huge combines driven by people who wave at me as I ride by. I sometimes stop by the road for the sheer joy of absorbing the smell of harvest, an indescribable fragrance, dry and seasoned yet tangy and sharp. After the combines whine down the road to other fields, red and yellow balers take over and efficiently bundle the leftover straw into neat bales as the setting sun lights up clouds of dust behind them.

Between me and the fields, the wild roses bloom first, then teasel and timothy and Queen Anne's Lace take over, waving like passing neighbors, and then the blackberries ripen in tangled profusion in the fence rows.

The fresh tastes and smells of summer are almost divine, as well – field-ripened strawberries first, then radishes from the garden. Fat blueberries from neighbor Dot Kropf's patch. Sweet cherries from Detering Orchards. Scents of fresh cilantro and tomato vines cling to my hands when I work in the garden. And one afternoon the children pick a bucketful of blackberries beside the road and I make the first blackberry pies of the season, the flavor so rich and delicious that I don't even mind the sticky purple drips on the bottom of my oven.

Summer is the season of expansion. Fragile petunia plants in my hanging pots balloon into green velvet clouds studded with bright purple jewels. The garden reaches in all directions, the corn leaping upward after a sluggish June, the zucchini growing seemingly overnight from little field mice to full-grown nutria. I turn my back for a couple of days, and the tomato plants become a jungle, tangled and thick, lacking only parrots and howler monkeys. And then one day, quite unexpectedly, when I get in the van and back it out from under the oak tree, I hear the unmistakable rattle of acorns rolling along the roof, a sure sign of fall. And I think, "Aack! Not yet! Summer has just started! Please, not yet!"

So this is my one complaint about summer in the Willamette Valley: It's far too short.

And the life of our family of eight seems to have reached its own summer season, as well: busy, growing, and productive. My boys are sacking grass seed in our warehouse this summer, coming home with dust in their eyebrows and green stains on their T-shirts, arms, and even necks from lifting hundreds of green-printed paper seed sacks.

I savor the tastes of this season—long late-night discussions with almost-adult children, laughter at family jokes. Most days, even during harvest, we manage to gather, all eight of us, around the table for supper. We hold hands to give thanks for the food, and I think, "Thank you most of all that we can all be here, together."

We are expanding in this season, not in number but in appetites and size. The two teenage boys seem to develop new arms and legs that fill the house like Alice in Wonderland when she drank from the magic bottle. Jenny, 8, is rapidly losing and replacing teeth and, it seems to me, determined to outgrow everything in her closet by next week. I cook food in large kettles and buy rice and flour in 50-pound sacks, eggs in boxes of five dozen. Huge pizzas disappear, gallons of iced tea and six-quart Crock-Pots brim full of roast beef and potatoes.

And like an Oregon summer, this season of our lives is passing too quickly.

My father-in-law, who was old, used to take a nap on the couch every afternoon during harvest. This year Paul, who does not at all seem old to me, announced that the time has come for him to do the same. With a cover on the couch to protect it from the warehouse-dust on his jeans, he snoozes with his nose in the air, just like his dad once did.

Jenny gets annoyed when I call her my baby, and she barely fits on my lap anymore. Emily is proud of her new driver's license and freedom. Matt is preparing for his transfer to the engineering program at Oregon State University this fall.

Our oldest daughter, Amy, will soon be off to a new job at a church school in South Carolina. Will Oregon's perfect summers call her back home? I wonder. I have no way of

27

knowing. Perhaps realizing that these seasons will pass soon is what makes them so precious. Maybe this taste of heaven is meant to whet our appetites for eternity. I don't know.

I just know that this summer, while the grapevines snake into the pine trees and the sun shines through the haze of ryegrass dust in the air, I see my son's suddenly huge feet, my daughter's suitcase, my husband's weariness, and I think, "Oh! But we just started! Please, not yet, not yet."

Shooting for Good-Mom Points

I went to my son's basketball game last week mostly out of guilt. Matt, who is 21, has been playing on a church-league team all winter. Even though he insisted it doesn't matter, and I don't enjoy basketball, I was feeling like a terrible mom for not attending his games. So on Tuesday evening I put lots of children in the car and drove 45 minutes to the high school in Lebanon.

Sitting in the cold gym, I tried dutifully to follow the action. What did it all mean—the raised fists, the sudden whistles, the constant motion? I managed to yell an enthusiastic "Yes!" when someone I knew made a basket, but was plunged into confusion when Matt's team suddenly started shooting at the wrong basket. It turns out they switch sides halfway through the game—how odd. At least I learned something new.

In contrast, my sister-in-law Bonnie, mother of the Harrisburg Eagles' Justin Smucker, has attended her sons' games for years and follows every detail with enthusiasm. She even knows what to yell. At the game in Lebanon she sat on the edge of her seat and shouted, not just a timid "Yes!" like me, but deep, insightful instructions such as "DE-fense!" "Wait till it's open!" "Let 'em foul you!" "Pass it!" and again, "DE-fense!"

What would it be like, I wondered in awe, to be such an expert mom that I knew something intelligent to holler at my child's basketball game?

One of the dark secrets of motherhood is that many of us keep "good-mom/bad-mom" balance sheets in our heads, one for ourselves and a smaller one for others. A "good-mom" mark on a friend's sheet generally means a "bad-mom" mark on ours, such as Bonnie and me at that basketball game.

The reverse is also true. A relative of mine told me recently how fortunate she is that the mothers of her children's friends are all terrible cooks, every one of them. This means that her kids and all their friends rave over her cooking, even if it's only a simple chicken stir-fry or spaghetti. I was envious, since my friends are all phenomenal cooks, but I was also happy for her, knowing how often she feels her scales are tipped to the other side.

My sister and I have been known to sit up late and tell endless mom-guilt stories, anguishing together. "I thought I should restrict his fluids since he was wetting the bed, so I didn't let him drink anything after supper for a few weeks, and then he got this terrible pain in his stomach and it turned out to be kidney stones. Oh, the guilt, I can't describe it."

My husband, Paul, walks by shaking his head in disbelief when we go on like this. His decisions, good or bad, are put in the past and left there, and he says I enjoy feeling guilty so much that when there's nothing handy to feel guilty about, I invent something, and then I feel guilty for feeling guilty.

His sister, Lois, reads parenting author John Rosemond and tells me kindly that I'm a classic American mom, constantly feeling that I'm not doing enough for my children. Despite what my husband and a few super-confident friends say, I think our angst is justified: We have invested heavily in this task, but we won't know until years from now what the returns will actually be.

This is the minefield of motherhood: We make a hundred decisions a day, large and small, often on the fly, using the best knowledge we have on hand, which usually isn't much, with only a guess as to the final results. In a classic "Stone Soup" comic strip, 12-year-old Holly yells, "I'm going to bring this up in therapy someday!" And this is our fear, that a moment's decision today will have terrible consequences 20 years from now.

A friend of mine was confronted by her adult son some time ago. She didn't let him get a motorcycle when he was 17, he said, and in doing so she destroyed something important in his soul. He was getting to be a man, and this was a man's decision, the first one, and so significant. She stole something valuable from him when she refused to let him experience this defining moment of manhood. He tried to be kind about this, and my friend tried hard to understand.

"But," she confided later, "how was I supposed to know? It seemed like he wasn't ready for it, at the time, and it wouldn't be safe. I had no idea that one thing would affect him like this, all these years later. And there's nothing I can do now."

My children, knowing my weakness, like to exploit the "bring this up in therapy" line. I laugh them off when the right choice is obvious, but it's the subtler things that keep me up at night.

For instance, I never expected to have children who were athletic, but I married a man whose genes proved dominant to mine, and we had to decide about involving the kids in sports. On the one hand, it takes a lot of time for parents, both in driving and watching. I am not a pleasant mom when I'm too busy; we all know this. We also know there are enormous benefits to having the whole family sitting down to supper every evening. On the other hand, team sports have benefits as well, and should we deny our children if all their friends are playing?

We finally decided to provide them plenty of equipment and chances to play with their friends, but organized sports would wait until they could drive themselves. Naturally, Paul never second-guessed this decision and I agonize regularly over it.

Our 14-year-old son, Ben, patted me on the shoulder after Matt's game and said, "Mom, I just want you to know that when I play basketball you won't have to feel like you're a bad mom if you don't come to my games." Then he added, "Now, it does matter to me if you come to my choir concerts or not." No problem there, at least. I wouldn't miss his concerts for anything.

Who knows, maybe all of Ben's friends will sit in therapy someday, weeping about their frazzled, competitive childhoods and how they always envied Ben for his fun, relaxed life.

Motherhood is a dangerous and dimly-lit path, and there are no guarantees. Some days the good-mom points outnumber the bad; some days not. But I move forward in faith and hope, trusting that my children will someday, as the book of Proverbs says, stay in the way they should go, and maybe even—Oh joy!—rise up and call their mother blessed.

Going Places

Adventures in Letting Go

*M*y husband planned our trip like NASA preparing a shuttle launch. Weather maps splashed across the computer screen: 6 a.m. Thursday—lime-green for rain in Oregon, lavender and pale blue for snow in Montana; noon—the colors shifted ominously to the right.

We needed to leave at 5 a.m. on Thursday, Paul finally decided, to get through Montana's high passes in daylight. Then he researched gasoline prices and planned our course, driving times, and gas stops—down to the quarter-hour— the 1,900 miles from Harrisburg to my parents' house near Grove City, Minnesota.

We knew the risks of driving this route in December. Yet, we felt we needed to have our children spend another Christmas with their grandparents, and flying a family of our size is much more expensive than loading us all into the van and driving.

How we snatch, at such times, at illusions of control. We were "minimizing the risks," we told ourselves, convinced that our charts, cellular phones, extra coats, an emergency kit under the seat, and Paul's expertise at driving in snow would somehow protect us if nature or chance turned against us.

We left right on time, stopping in Portland to pick up my 15-year-old niece, Hillary, then heading east on Interstate 84, conquering the miles. Kennewick, Coeur d'Alene, Butte.

Except for one unscheduled restroom break that annoyed Paul more than all the hours of noise and bickering in the back seats, we kept to the charts, arriving in Minnesota on Friday afternoon.

Coming back home was different. Sudden freezing rain in Minnesota and snow and wind in the Dakotas forced us to change our route. Like rungs of a ladder, the interstate highways cross the column of Midwestern states, and we had to drive many miles south, to the third rung down, Interstate 80 in Nebraska, to escape the storms.

None of our careful planning included creeping down a mountain on the snowy shoulder of I-80 in western Wyoming while the black ice on the pavement reflected the dusky sky. Enormous trucks that had roared past, splashing dirty water on our windshield, now crawled meekly or lay on their sides in the median, lights still on, pathetically helpless and disturbingly twisted. Nature is king in the wilds of Wyoming, following its own course despite all our plans and calculations.

In much the same way, I have found, the people in our lives resist our presumptuous attempts at prediction, at taming, at bending to our will. From the first pregnancy to our parents' last years, we grasp at illusions of control. We gather our tools—charts, research, and all the right books. We convince ourselves, in 1990 or 1995, that we know how things ought to be in 2009, and that with knowledge and discipline we can make it happen.

My mother was always busy and hardworking. I expected her, by age 85, to let others clean and cook and to do only what she does best: reading to the grandchildren, writing letters, sending cheerful cards, and making Bible-verse scrapbooks for people.

Instead, she is determined to work as hard as she did 30 years ago. "No, no, I can do that!" she said when I told our lanky 19-year-old, Matt, to take out the garbage or bring in the card table for Christmas dinner. She labored over the sink, slicing apples for grandchildren who, in my opinion, have perfectly good teeth and can bite into whole apples.

If I resisted her attempts to tell me how to grow up, why do I expect her to listen to me tell her how to grow old?

After Christmas, Matt caught a bus to Indiana to begin a six-week term at a Bible school. He is a smart, responsible young man who is nevertheless a bit dangerous, saying exactly what he thinks, wearing only what's comfortable, and doing stupid things on a dare.

"Behave yourself," I said, telling him goodbye. "Don't wear that dreadful black hooded sweatshirt that makes you look like the Grim Reaper."

"But it's comfortable, and it's going to be cold there," he answered quietly, with that calm, dismissive attitude my husband displays when his mom worries about him sleeping by an open window.

I pictured Matt wearing the same clothes for days on end and wondered what the girls would think. I don't want him to start dating yet, but it was small comfort to know that his clothing habits are not likely to impress any young ladies.

But then, who can predict young ladies? The two 15-year-olds in our van, Hillary and our daughter Emily, chose their words and behavior by some invisible standard that I could neither guide nor understand. Neither one, for instance, wore socks. All of my logical lectures made no difference. They scampered into gas stations over ice, in rain, and through blowing snow with bare feet in tennis shoes (Emily) or skimpy black dress shoes with little bows (Hillary).

Hillary's mother and I have tried to raise our daughters to be strong and confident young women. But at 15, Emily screams and Hillary apologizes. A waitress handed Hillary an ice cream cone. She took it, squeezing too hard, and the cone began to collapse in her hand. Emily screamed. Every head in the restaurant swiveled. Hillary, embarrassed, apologized shyly.

From inside an Idaho Flying J restroom, I heard the loudest scream of the whole trip. I came out and the girls, giggling, pointed to a little brown refrigerator with a big pink sign: "WORMS $1.99"

"What happened?"

"OK, we're out here waiting, and Hillary goes, 'Hmmm, worms?' and opens the door, and there's all these little round blue plastic containers. So she picks one up and opens it, and it's like, full of these live, writhing blueish-purple worms! So I was like, 'AAAHHH!'"

"What did you expect? I mean, it said, 'Worms.'"

"I thought they'd be dead and pink."

"I'm sorry I literally opened a can of worms," Hillary murmured, eyes downcast. She lives near Portland, but I told her she is actually a true Midwesterner, a person who apologizes when someone steps on her foot.

Which is more scary, to see the ones I love choose their own paths or to sit in the front seat, stomach tight with anxiety, wondering if the next quarter-mile of slick highway will send us plunging down a Wyoming mountainside? At that moment, eyeing the overturned trucks was worse.

Paul drove, stiff and grim, and I calculated whether we would hit a truck or roll down the embankment if we lost control right here. Evening descended, cold and ominous. The children were unusually quiet.

Emily's voice spoke up from the back, calm and sure. "The Lord is my shepherd, I shall not want." One by one, the others joined in. "He maketh me to lie down in green pastures; he leadeth me beside the still waters." Despite the danger, a pervasive sense of peace surrounded us.

Signs for a motel appeared in the endless Wyoming wasteland. We crept to the next exit and pulled safely into the parking lot. With its red carpet, extra pillows, and fancy little shampoos, our room was far more classy than the normal motels we patronize.

"This," Emily crowed, exploring, "is an adventure!"

A lesson in faith from my screaming, sockless 15-year-old: a life tidy and managed has no adventure; a tightly controlled relationship no joy. I could loosen my rigid grasp and trust the shepherd to bring us safely home.

And late the next evening, he did.

No Longer Young, Thank God

There's nothing like being surrounded by a hundred teenagers to make you happy to be on the other side of 40.

My husband, Paul, and I were recently asked to speak at a Mennonite church youth retreat in northern Idaho. This annual event drew young people from four neighboring states and even a few from Pennsylvania and Ohio.

Parenting three teenagers is one thing; interacting with dozens of them for an entire weekend is quite another. We talked to them in the sanctuary, ate with them in a noisy cafeteria, and watched them play endless rounds of volleyball.

"This makes me feel young," Paul said, "and it makes me feel old."

All weekend I had flashbacks to the last time I attended a similar event. It was more than 25 years ago, when I was about 17, and two carloads of us from Minnesota drove down to the youth fellowship meetings in Kalona, Iowa. Both then and now, I was fascinated with the complicated dynamics at play in such a group—the rituals, the interplay, the subtle competitions under the surface. I fancied myself an amateur Margaret Mead, analyzing it all. How things change, I decided. And how they stay the same.

The biggest difference was that back then, I was a teenager, and in the middle of it all, obsessing about my hair, evaluating the guys, and feeling dowdy next to the girls who showed up more fashionably dressed than I. Now, in contrast, I could observe, comfortable and amused, from the distance of 20-some years.

The behavior of girls and guys in a large group, I decided, has not changed a bit. Girls meeting long-lost friends go through a little ritual that played out over and over as the carloads arrived: A wild, feminine squeal, "ASHLEEEEEEE!" that could be heard all over the gym and fellowship room was followed by an exuberant hug and shrill laughter.

As a teenager, I nearly drowned in embarrassment when I spotted my out-of-state cousin across a crowded gym and shrieked her name, and everyone turned and—horrors!—looked at me. Such impulsive exhibition—I must be some sort of freak, I thought. This time, as I watched similar scenes repeated in front of me, I wished I could go back and tell myself how normal I actually was, that this simply is what girls do.

In the church cafeteria in Idaho, the guys and girls congregated at separate tables and peeled the foil off their hot sandwiches. The girls ate daintily and engaged in happy conversation while the guys slyly checked out the girls, then wolfed down their sandwiches, wadded up the foil, and threw it at their friends. The established couples ate together shyly at little tables off to the side.

Paul and I seemed very old and very married in contrast. He felt no compulsion to toss tin foil balls to impress me, and I had no need to giggle to get his attention. Usually we ate together, but if he was busy talking with people, I went through the line and ate by myself without feeling any less secure in our relationship.

There's a certain exciting suspense to life, my daughters inform me, until you find the Right One. The Thrill of the

Chase, my sister, Margaret, used to call it, and she wondered if she'd miss it after she was married.

Surrounded by the mostly subtle interaction around us, I exchanged amused glances across the table with Paul and decided that being settled with the Right One and having all that angst behind me is just fine, thank you very much.

Most of the girls at the retreat wore "cape" dresses, the uniform of many Amish and some Mennonite churches, a simple dress with an extra piece of fabric over the bodice from shoulder to waist. I wore capes growing up and was often told that their purpose is to free women from the tyranny of changing fashions. But fashion must be hardwired into the feminine genes because even cape dresses pass through their own distinct trends and phases.

Back in Iowa at the fellowship meetings of my youth, all the cool, intimidating Indiana girls showed up with gathers on their sleeves, their waists, their necklines, and their yokes, and most of these gathers were embellished with little fabric bows. No one from our area had as yet dared to try these, so we looked on in envy and felt backward and plain.

How times have changed. Gathers are as out as polyester doubleknit. The current look is straight and sleek, from neck to waist and down to the hem. "Mid-calf" was the prescribed length for us, back in our day, and we convinced ourselves of very loose definitions for "mid" and "calf" so that most of our dresses were not far below the knee. At this retreat, not a single dress was shorter than the dictionary-definition mid-calf. To my amusement, the cutting-edge girls from the East played volleyball in dresses that brushed their shoetops.

But then, who was I to chuckle at these young ladies? After all, I wore a navy-blue, long-sleeved, polyester double-knit dress with a three-inch-wide belt to the fellowship meetings on a hot, humid Iowa night—because I was convinced it made me look elegant, and it was as cool, in fashion if not temperature, as I could get.

While I still wear dresses, I no longer wear capes on them, and on the first evening of the retreat I cheerfully wore a green corduroy dress that I bought at Goodwill a few years ago. How freeing to know that I now can use a dress until it actually wears out without worrying about fitting in. Looking back, it seems my life was fraught with anxiety, drama, and taking things much too seriously. I was still shopping for a personality, and laughing at myself at 17 was not an option.

Today, I know all too well who I am. With my children and their friends poking fun at my absentmindedness and other quirks, I might as well join in.

I laughed with everyone else when my niece Jessi recounted how their carload passed ours on the way to Idaho. "There was this big van, and there's little Aunt Dorcas, driving and driving, with earbuds in her ears, just ignoring everything around her. We drove beside them for a long time and waved and waved and tried to get her attention, but she just drove and drove and didn't even notice us." Jessi included an accurate imitation: hands on a big imaginary steering wheel, nose up, eyes staring straight ahead, oblivious to the world.

"Your choices accumulate," I told the girls in my hour-long talk to them on Saturday afternoon. "Even the small things add up to a pile that becomes your life when you're my age." They listened, smiling and attentive, 59 young

women who seemed determined to choose the right mate-
rials to construct their lives.

Youth, I concluded, is nice in its own way—the energy, the
exciting opportunities, the freedom, the ability to program a
cell phone, the astonishing metabolism. But ultimately I am
glad to be on this side of 40, with the big questions answered
and the major decisions settled.

I don't plan to dye my expanding crop of gray hair or
buy expensive lotions to plump up my wrinkles. I've earned
every single one, and I would not be a teenager again for all
the fancy dresses in the world.

Discovering Ben

*R*ight from the beginning, mothering involves discovering who this child is.

"What is it like when you give birth and first see your baby?" my daughter, Emily, asked me not long ago. I told her, "Of course you're just thrilled, and then you feel like, 'Oh! So that was you in there all that time! I knew there was somebody but I didn't know it was YOU.'" She thought that was funny. But that is how it was, every time, and I found it doesn't stop at birth but continues constantly as a mom explores who her children really are and then helps them find out the same for themselves.

As part of this process, I take each child on a one- or two-day excursion when they're 12, known in our family vernacular as their "Twelve Trip"; my husband takes them on a longer "Thirteen Trip" the next year. With six children and a swarm of responsibilities, our emphasis is on functioning as a group. These trips help us focus on each child alone, outside the context of a large family.

Ben, our second son and fourth child, didn't mind that his trips were reversed. He and Paul went camping in Yosemite for a week last summer. He and I decided to go to Bend after the snow melted in the mountains.

So while Ben was discovering Bend last weekend, I was busy rediscovering Ben. Of course I already knew that Ben is a likable and brainy young man who enjoys nature and sports and dislikes shopping, which is why I suggested Central Oregon as a destination and not the outlet malls in Lincoln City.

I picked him up after school in Brownsville and we headed east. In Sweet Home, I pulled in at an espresso stand to treat him to a fruit smoothie. Twelve Trips allow indulgences made impractical at other times by voices hollering from the back seats: "Can I have one, too? That's not fair!"

To my surprise, he shrugged. "Naaah, you don't need to."

"Really?"

"Yeah, I don't really want anything."

I thought, "Amazing," and, "How different from his sisters."

It seems things that matter terribly to his siblings don't bother Ben at all—a worrisome trait. What if I have produced a child without much personality? Or, even more troubling, what if he has deep feelings that he doesn't know how to communicate?

Yet he does have his passions, including geography, the outdoors, and facts and figures. Driving through the Cascade Mountains east of Sweet Home, he said, pointing, "That's the Calapooia River. And over that ridge there is the Marcola Valley. And the Santiam is a little ways that way, kind of north."

"How do you know this stuff?" I asked.

"Oh, from observation. And from studying the atlas."

As stunning views of Mount Washington and Three-Fingered Jack appeared through the trees, Ben kept asking me to pull over. Swinging his camera, he trotted back along the guardrail so he could frame the mountain peak between two trees, just right.

His older brother, Matt, I recalled, loved nature as well and stayed awake nights worrying about endangered species. Ben loves nature by going out and enjoying it. Having a less complicated child is not a bad thing, I decided.

I treated him to pizza at Izzy's when we got to Bend. He would have been equally happy with dollar-menu hamburgers at McDonalds, but he let me think I was doing something special for him.

At our motel, he flopped blissfully back onto the four fat pillows on his bed and began to read *Great Moments in Baseball History*. Contented and easy to please—this is a good thing as well.

The next day, I forced myself to bypass tempting fluorescent green garage sale signs and focus on what Ben would enjoy. First, a visit to the top of Pilot Butte in the middle of town, where a circular engraved metal plate pointed us toward the peaks on the horizon. We are both sign-readers and information gatherers. "OK, so that's the North Sister over there, and it's 25.4 miles away. And that perfectly symmetrical mountain there is Black Butte. And that mountain there is actually smaller than the South Sister but it looks bigger because it's 4.6 miles closer."

Why is it, I wondered, that Ben and I get along so well? Our only disagreement of the morning was at the High Desert Museum: Should we hang around to listen to this old-fashioned group sing "Clementine" and other folk songs? We compromised: one song, and then we wandered through the pioneer section and were equally intrigued with realistic displays of a covered wagon and the Oregon Trail. Ben was interested in the statistics of pioneer life; I wanted to weep for the women who wore "dun-colored" sunbonnets so they wouldn't show the dust of the trail and who buried children along the way.

Is it a bad trait for Ben to have so few feelings? I wondered. Back in the car I began to probe. What is he thinking, are there things he wishes he could tell me, what does he hope for the future, is he worried about anything?

Three minutes of this was enough. "Mom, why are you asking me all this stuff anyway?"

I sighed. "Because good moms talk about heavy things when they're alone with their kids." He chuckled, "Hey, did you hear about the guy who could bench-press 2,400 pounds?" I gave up.

Then we hiked for a long time, along an old logging railroad grade to a waterfall on the Deschutes River, and over a huge lava field covered with rough black rocks and ominous gullies where a mountain blew up long ago and where astronauts once practiced for the first moonwalk.

Then, under the hot sun, a light-bulb moment for me: Ben is a replica of his dad. That explains everything—the contentment, the calm, the scarcity of emotions, the abundance of action, the preference for planning and doing over talking and feeling, the barrels of facts in his brain. That also explains why we get along so well. And, a thought to put off for another day: Why do I get along best with the children who are least like me?

Halfway through the lava field I was so tired I thought my knees would collapse, but Ben was eager for more. Up ahead was Lava Butte, a 500-foot-high hump with gravelly sides that sloped upward at what seemed an 89-degree angle.

"I'd like to climb that," he said. "You can wait around here somewhere if you want." I let him go on ahead, guessing correctly that there was no way to get there from the trail. He came jogging back, only mildly disappointed. "We need to come back sometime and figure out how to get up there."

"Yes," I said. "We do. Maybe this summer."

This is my job: to guide and encourage him so he has the tools to do his job, which is this: to discover himself, to discover the world, and possibly to someday repeat this journey of discovery with a child of his own.

Rivers of the Soul

My daughter looked worried. "But Mom, you haven't been in the back of a canoe for—what? Years?"

"It's like riding a bike: You never forget," I said flippantly, too preoccupied with packing marshmallows and matches to wonder if I actually remembered the finer points of J-strokes from our long-ago years of roughing it in northwestern Ontario. In a two-person canoe, the front person's job is straightforward: paddle. The person in the rear bears most of the responsibility for steering the canoe.

I was about to join my husband and children on an overnight canoe trip down the Willamette River. When Paul took the boys two years ago, he didn't realize he was starting a June tradition. The next year, our teenaged daughters joined them. Eight-year-old Jenny wanted to go this year, and Paul preferred not to take her unless I was along as well—which meant that I had a decision to make.

I stayed home the last two years because the greatest treat for a mom of many is not to go away somewhere, but to have the house all to herself. Also, I prefer civilized vacations.

Roughing it is fine for the guys, who like to sit around the campfire, gnaw on meat, and grunt like Neanderthals, unshaven and unshowered. But I appreciate scented soaps and deep mattresses. Yet, previously, even while I sewed without interruption, I often second-guessed myself. Were laziness and inertia and fear keeping me from fun and adventure and making memories?

So I decided: This year, I would go along, not only for Jenny's sake but also to make sure I wasn't missing out on something. Since I was more experienced than the boys, Paul wanted me in the back of Ben's canoe.

We put in at Marshall Island, south of Junction City— seven people, three canoes, and roughly as many supplies as Lewis and Clark took up the Missouri. As soon as we pushed off, I realized three things: The determined current of the Willamette was a whole other category of water than the lakes and rivers of Ontario; I had a well-meaning but oblivious teenager in front; and I had forgotten everything I ever knew about managing a canoe, including which hand was left or right.

The others were soon stroking efficiently up ahead of us as I sweated through the complicated maneuvers—pushing out, pulling in—and shouted at Ben to just paddle and quit trying to steer from up there. Old tree roots stuck out of the water, perilous sieves threatening to pull us in as we zigzagged clumsily by. Strange currents pushed us sideways and dangerous-looking swirls on the water seemed to flaunt their power over me.

Before long my arm throbbed from shoulder to fingertips with an extreme version of the tendonitis that often afflicts my wrists. If a few tears dripped into the Willamette, we will not mention it here, but I kept going, determined to conquer this challenge if it was the last thing I did.

This is the trouble with new adventures: They take you to unexplored territory of the soul as well. You find out things about yourself you'd just as soon not know, things you don't have to face when you stay home and piece quilts.

Why, for instance, do I have this enormous fear of being thought weak and wimpy? Never mind that I actually am weak and wimpy; I just don't want anyone else to think so. And why, I wondered, furiously paddling, would I rather stomp off and quit entirely than admit that this isn't working and ask if we can rearrange?

My thoughts churned on: Why am I just like my mother, who at 87 won't ask for help with anything, including washing windows and cleaning gutters? Desperately pushing on, as pain screeched up and down my arm, I wondered what possessed me to put myself into a situation that exposed my weakest areas and worst faults.

Paul is not one to grasp subtle nuances, but my demeanor must have somehow told him things weren't going too well. We stopped to rest at a gravel bar near the railroad bridges. "How are you doing?" he asked, so kind and concerned that I resented it, because sympathy does me in every time, including this one.

Paul is often amazed at how he has to spell out the obvious. "You actually have the option of saying that this isn't working and could we rearrange," he said, wisely refraining from stating the also-obvious—that I carry bravery and determination to insane extremes.

So I ended up in the front of a canoe, with 17-year-old Emily in the back. My arm and outlook slowly improved as we worked our way north through Harrisburg. Emily is excellent at managing a canoe, but neither of us is very strong, so we were still the last stragglers.

Patiently, Paul rearranged us all again and put me in the front of his canoe, which improved everything. Paul called our oldest son, Matt, on his cell phone, and he met us at the McCartney Park boat landing with the wrist braces that I wear for typing. Then it no longer hurt as much to paddle, and slowly the world righted itself as the smell of the river and calm green of the trees dissolved the tension in my tortured soul.

We ate supper on a poppy-covered bar. Paul grilled burgers while I laid ketchup and plates on the plastic tablecloth that the girls had poked fun at me for bringing along. "Eating is more efficient when Mom's along," Amy observed. Paul told me, generously, "Everything's less chaotic when you're along."

Two hours downriver, we set up our tents on a mysterious island with tall bushes and oversized morning glories. Jenny appointed herself Official Wood Gatherer, and scavenged armloads of driftwood. Then, to my surprise, she expertly arranged the wood in a careful teepee—broken bits of kindling below, larger pieces above, air pockets here and there—as though she had been building campfires all her life. We lit it and it burned, just as a proper campfire ought to.

This is the nice thing about new adventures—they expose skills and talents you never knew you had. Emily, for instance, is far from athletic. Yet when she and Paul first went canoeing on Muddy Creek, about four years ago, they discovered her remarkable knack for handling a canoe. "My strategy," Emily says confidently, "is to avoid the funny-looking water."

Steven grabbed the fishing gear as soon as the canoes were unloaded and precisely cast and reeled in until long after it grew dark and the rest of us were relaxing around Jenny's campfire.

The next day, on a calm stretch of water, we put the two boys in a canoe by themselves and were happily surprised at how soon they caught on to navigating it. The rest of the day was simply fun: alternately drifting with the current and paddling, watching ospreys, listening to the children singing Veggie-Tales songs and "The Star-Spangled Banner," and waving at a farmer on the bank.

Before we knew it, we saw the houses and church steeple of Peoria, where Matt met us and we piled our smoky bags and pillows in the back of the van and loaded the canoes on the trailer.

"So, are you glad now that you went?" Amy asked me a few days later.

"Yes," I said, not only because I knew that's what she wanted to hear, but because I really meant it.

When the next opportunity for adventure comes along, I hope I have the courage to leave my calm familiar backwaters and again launch into the unknown currents of the soul.

Three "Girls" Cross the Country

We were ready to conquer the country, so to speak. Amy's massive suitcase took up most of the trunk; half the back seat was piled high with supplies. We hugged the others goodbye and were on our way.

In the pocket of the passenger-side door, I found a pink-and-green striped notebook titled "The Shotgun Soliloquy." "Anyone who sits there can write in it," Amy explained. I pulled the pale green pen out of the black wire binding and wrote:

"July 30, 2007. Off we go on a girls' adventure—me, Amy, Emily. Off to Ohio, Pennsylvania, and South Carolina—loaded with suitcases, paperwork, iced tea, food, pillows, and expectation."

Amy is 19; Emily two years younger. We have done many things together—going to garage sales, teaching Vacation Bible School, and processing sweet corn for the freezer with efficient teamwork. But we had never considered undertaking anything as extensive as driving across the country.

Amy had accepted a job offer at a church school in South Carolina, and she needed her car there. A nephew was getting married in Pennsylvania in August, the girls wanted to attend a church convention in Ohio, and my publisher was eager to arrange signings in the East for my new book.

My husband, Paul, is the family organizer. "I think the three of you should drive out," he said, "and then the rest of us can fly out for the wedding."

Drive? Three non-mechanical females? For thousands of miles?

"You'll be fine," Paul said, and so I somehow knew we would be, even though for the last 25 years I have gratefully let him be in charge of our road trips.

We left on a Monday afternoon, the last bags nestled around our feet. "Mom is so proud of herself for having only one suitcase, but then she has like *five* purses!" Amy muttered.

We had three-and-one-half days to cover the 2,400 miles to Ohio. Two missed roads put us behind schedule, and our first difference of opinion occurred at Burns. The girls wanted to kick back at a motel. I wanted to push on to Ontario. I gave in, grudgingly, and for the first time understood my husband's irritating conquer-the-miles insistence when we travel.

At a rest stop just after we crossed into Idaho on Tuesday morning, Amy popped the hood and pulled out the dipstick. In the blazing sunlight, it was almost impossible to tell if the little holes had a film of oil over them or not. Amy finally decided they did not, and poured in another half quart of oil.

"Women find a trip with best friends and no menfolk is a relaxing, empowering experience," announced a feature in *The Register-Guard* some time ago. There was, indeed, something empowering about learning the skills we had always left to Paul. Later that day I taught Amy how to pump her own gas, something she had had no chance to learn in Oregon.

We navigated the mountainous northeast corner of Utah in a steady rain and entered the interminable desolation of Wyoming. "Wyoming brings out my inner teenager," I told

Paul on the phone after several hours of cruising at the speed limit of 75 miles per hour. To stay awake as we approached Laramie late that night, we took turns making up verses to "She'll be comin' round the mountain," such as "We'll be comin' into Laramie, but that really doesn't scare me."

The three of us are more different than alike, but we blend well. Amy and I try to motivate Emily, who, like a toy car on cheap batteries, has short-lived bursts of energy that quickly run out. The girls attempt to pull me into the 21st century, telling me to untuck my shirts and tone down the "pouf" in my hair. And Emily and I try to loosen up Amy who is sometimes too sensible and thrifty for her own good.

Somewhere around Nebraska it began to dawn on us that if all went well, this was actually less about grand adventure and more about just plain hard slogging, hour after hour. We stopped to sleep and took brief breaks; otherwise we simply drove, with virtually no drama or memorable events.

Actually, the most dramatic event of the trip was when Emily suddenly screamed and flailed her arms in front of Amy, who was driving. "Emily, stop that! What on Earth?" I said.

"A moth!" she shrieked, swatting at the windshield.

"A moth isn't worth dying for," Amy snapped.

The long mother-daughter talks I had hoped for never materialized, as it seemed that whoever wasn't driving was sleeping or studying the atlas or reading. However, we spent hours listening together to *Chronicles of Narnia* CDs, the fantasy-land of the story contrasting with the cornfields of Nebraska and Iowa.

A steamy heat covered the Midwest. We Oregonians, accustomed to air with oxygen in it, felt half smothered whenever we ventured outside. In Iowa, the air-conditioner fan quit and we drove with the windows open, the moist air whipping across our faces.

By the next day, mercifully, the fan worked again, but Emily wrote in the Shotgun Soliloquy: "Once upon a time a starving monster went to Indiana and realized that there, the people were already cooked. 'Yum Yum,' he said. But soon he, too, was cooked in the insane heat. That was the end of the starving giant. Note to self: If you fall in love with someone from Indiana, convince him to move to Oregon."

On the fourth day, we finally reached Ohio and the home of Paul's nephew, Kevin, and his wife. Over the supper table, we recounted our journey. Kevin was impressed with our fearless sense of adventure.

The worst driving came after our weekend in Ohio, when we followed Interstate 76, narrow and twisting, to eastern Pennsylvania. Like a rabbit caught in a buffalo stampede, I maneuvered our little Civic among hundreds of huge trucks, through rain and road construction and single-lane bottle-necks, thinking nostalgically of wide-open Wyoming.

We reached my sister's house at last. The other family members joined us, we saw the nephew get married, the books were signed, and the rest flew home. On the final leg of our journey, Amy and I drove to South Carolina, the accents and tea getting thicker and sweeter as we headed south. By the time we reached her new home, we had covered 4,000 miles.

I wrote in the Shotgun Soliloquy: "How to drive across the country: Get in the car. Drive and drive. How to reach big goals: Start. Work and work."

Amy left me at the airport the next day where I cried the sort of tears that only a parent understands.

The real adventure has been the past 19 years; the best thing has been the journey itself. The accomplishment was not so much driving across the country as it was having two daughters who didn't hesitate to get in the car with their 40-something mother to do so, and I count myself blessed and successful.

Romance in Florida

At first glance, it couldn't get more romantic than this: leaving rainy Oregon in the middle of a long winter for a trip to Florida, just my husband and me, and right over Valentine's Day.

However, the rose of anticipation was wilted a bit by the fact that the trip's purpose was actually an "Enrichment Weekend" for Mennonite ministers. We would spend our time not sunbathing on the beach but, with a hundred other couples of the button-down shirt/homemade dress variety, listening to lectures on such dreamy subjects as "The Pastor as Biblical Counselor."

But the fact remained that this still was a trip to Florida, and I was determined to make the most of it. My wise neighbor and friend, Anita, has an enduring philosophy that comes up whenever we discuss marriage or our adult children or life in general. "Be thankful for what is," says Anita, "instead of complaining about what is not."

After 23 years of marriage, I am well aware of both. Daily life is mostly realism and responsibility, and Paul is not a poetry-reciting, roses-in-his-teeth sort of person. He is a steady, practical man who installs a new bathroom sink and hopes desperately that I will say that this counts as my birthday gift so he won't have to buy me anything.

So, while I am grateful that things are good, I also like to make them better. Could a busy, long-married, many-childrened pair of opposites headed for a pastors' seminar still manage to stir up the embers of romance? It was worth a try. And even if that didn't happen, I was determined to extract all the enjoyment the trip could offer.

There are people, I am told, who do not have children and can just pack up and leave on weekend trips. We, on the other hand, had to arrange rides to school, post lists of duties (Feed the cat! Turn off lights! Get the mail!), plan meals, find someone to stay overnight with the children, and sign medical-decision permission slips.

Paul was patient with my last-minute stress and then, driving to Portland, he deliberately chose to talk with me instead of shouting into his cell phone all the way about seed tests and how many loads of rice bran to haul to Kropf Feed while he was gone. I appreciated this.

On the plane, I pulled a *Spirit* magazine out of the seat pocket and read a wonderful article entitled "There Must Be 50 Ways to Woo Your Lover" about a practical, economizing man's attempts to romance his wife—on a trip to Florida, no less.

It was perfect for Paul, who never reads this sort of thing, but ought to.

I poked him. "Hey, there's something on page 64 of this magazine that you might want to read." Then I tucked it back in the pocket without pushing my point further, and went to sleep, snuggled on his shoulder. I have learned a few clever management techniques in 23 years.

Following a long layover in Las Vegas, we boarded the plane, which was shaking so much I started to feel sick. Finally the pilot announced that 84-mile-per-hour winds and lots of debris were flying down the runway, so we couldn't leave.

I rested my head and slept on Paul's lap, one of the many perks of traveling with a husband, until we finally took off, three hours late, which meant that we arrived, exhausted, in Tampa after 3 a.m. Naturally, as a frugal Mennonite minister, Paul had reserved an economy car. However, those were all taken, so we had three choices, all for the economy price: a sedate minivan, an SUV, or a Mitsubishi Spyder convertible. This was a terrible moral dilemma for a Mennonite minister—two large gas guzzlers vs. a worldly sports car.

Stewardship and gas mileage won out, and we sank into the convertible, kayak-like, and took off to find our hotel. Paul had indulged me by reserving a three-star room and satisfied his conscience by getting a fantastic deal on Priceline. There was only one problem: We couldn't find the hotel. Paul had directions and a map, but neither correlated with actual freeway signs, and as we swung past endless road construction and the clock inched toward 5 a.m., the last bubbles of romance popped from our exhausted minds and we stewed in irritation and near-despair.

Paul finally reached the right Hyatt Hotel on the phone and a nice woman talked us in: "Turn right at PetCo, OK, past the Denny's," and there we were at last. She told us we could extend the normal checkout time to 2 p.m., and we fell asleep and woke up many hours later in a beautiful room with brilliant sunshine edging the drapes. I made coffee in the little machine and all was well once again.

Later that afternoon we headed down to Sarasota in our Spyder and Paul, of his own volition, stopped so we could take a romantic walk on the beach. We arrived at the church early, so Paul put the car top down and we leaned back and napped in the sunshine. When I woke up, squinting, a pink envelope was propped on the gearshift beside me. He remembered Valentine's Day! With a card! With extra stuff written in it! "I like to spend time with you," the card said, and I was perfectly happy.

I gushed gratefully, and he grinned. "That ought to be worth two or three points." Hey, he must have actually read that article on the plane while I was asleep! My cup of joy ran over.

Our marriage has resulted in six children whom we love dearly but enjoy getting away from now and then. We found, however, that the tether that joins us stretches clear across the country, thanks to cell phones. Mine buzzed frantically in the middle of an evening service. I checked the caller—"Home"—and sensed that this was something bad—vomiting children, a broken leg, maybe a dead dog. I wanted to rush out to take the call, but our pew had about as much leg room as a coach seat on Southwest Airlines. There were six adults to my right and one very large one to my left, so I was stuck.

As I sweated through the speaker's closing comments, the phone buzzed twice more and I was certain the house was on fire, Jenny was kidnapped, or someone had totaled the van. Immediately after the last "Amen" I wormed out through the crowd and called home in a panic. Fourteen-year-old Ben answered. "Oh, Mom, it's you. Hey, when you're making spaghetti, do you boil the water before you put the spaghetti in?" I yelled at him, I admit, and Ben, a replica of his dad, was completely bewildered at my alarm.

The night before we left Florida, we lowered the car top again and drove out to the beach as the sun was setting and the warm breezes blew. "Maybe people will think that you're really rich and I'm your trophy wife," I told Paul.

And Paul, who I think is predictable but who actually never stops surprising me, replied, "You're my trophy wife whether people think so or not."

And then we flew home, where the daffodils were starting to bloom, which means that winter is officially over no matter what the calendar says, and I am thankful, as my friend Anita advises, for what has been, and for what is, and for what is yet to be.

Visiting my Amish Past

I've noticed that when my husband's relations gather at Kropf reunions, the ones who have strayed furthest from their Mennonite heritage rhapsodize the most about its value. I reflected on this during my recent experience of following eastern Iowa's muddy country roads back into my Amish past.

How much of that unique way of life have I lost? I wondered, as I confidently drove our rented Subaru Outback and gushed like a tourist about those adorable Amish children and the quaint navy-blue dresses on the clothesline. And how much have I kept? I also wondered, surprised at how easily I clicked back into discussing gardens and babies and family trees in Pennsylvania German.

My parents lived in the large Amish community of Kalona, Iowa, for a number of years in the 1950s and '60s. Four of us children were born there; Dad taught in the Amish schools. Mom and Dad now live in Minnesota but still have many relatives and connections in the Kalona area. My brother, Marcus, drives them the seven hours to Kalona now and then for funerals and such, but he seldom has time for the leisurely visiting that Mom and Dad enjoy. So my sister, Rebecca, and I came up with a plan: We would both fly to Minnesota—she from Virginia, I from Oregon—and we would take Mom and Dad to Iowa, wherever they wanted to go, to do all the visiting they wished.

Astonishingly, despite a family on each coast and Mom and Dad's precarious health in the middle, our plan worked out. Stocked with pillows and Mom's bag of homemade snacks, we headed south on Interstate 35. We headquartered at Aunt Vina's house and made meandering forays around town, to the nursing home to see Uncle Mahlon and down A Avenue to see where we used to live, and on out into the countryside, on roads sticky as rubber cement from the recent rains, to one quiet Amish home after another.

Dad's 100-year-old friend, Joe, sat at the dining room table wearing thick black-rimmed glasses, reading his German Bible with light from the window, since the gas lights aren't lit until dusk. Joe's two unmarried daughters care for him, keep the house immaculate, and run a fabric store next door. Rebecca and I browsed its dim interior, among baby bibs and black polyester, while a buggy and a patient horse waited outside. And then a voice said, "Who do I hear out there?" and out from behind a rack of fabric came my sweet cousin, Katie, and her husband, Harley, shopping for suspender clips, and we had a warm reunion right there at the cutting counter.

"Glen Beachys are next," Mom said, referring to their old friends in that Amish and Mennonite way of pluralizing the male head of the household to include the whole family. We pulled in and melted in awww's as we saw a dozen small children—boys in straw hats and homemade pants and shirts; girls in dresses and white organdy head-coverings— playing around the swing set. A small boy in a gray shirt grabbed the cross-bar at the end and swung energetically, knees bent, his bare feet pointing stiffly out behind.

Mrs. Beachy greeted us at the door, and suddenly people appeared on all sides. Women came from the kitchen, teenage girls looked over their mothers' shoulders, children wandered in from outside, men stopped tearing up the dining room linoleum and stood to welcome us. "We all came home to have a work day for Mom and Dad," explained a daughter. And there, suddenly, was Priscilla, now a Beachy daughter-in-law, who was my best friend when I was 4 years old, and who somehow looked just like she did back then, dark-eyed and smiling.

We felt like royalty as we gathered on the deck, their projects abandoned for, they implied, the joy and honor of having us there. There was no rush, no hints of unfinished work waiting, no hidden glances at pocket watches. Dad caught up on news of his former students while out on the lawn a small child held a doll in one hand and played with the dog with the other.

Later, at my cousin Perry's house, his wife, Rebecca, told us about their egg business, their 5,000 chickens, and their teenage son who spends most of the morning gathering eggs. And they also milk cows, she mentioned off-handedly. Forty of them, as I recall. While we talked, their daughter sat in the semi-darkness of the kitchen, cutting up apples to make applesauce.

At another house, a barefooted woman, mother of 12 children, paused in her work of canning meat for her daughter's wedding to take us across the road to visit with her elderly father. I asked about the boxes of onions piled in the shed. "We grow produce for a co-op," she said. "And we also milk 200 goats."

I confess I had expected the trip to be a bit boring, dutifully driving Mom and Dad from one house to the next along corn-lined gravel roads. I had no idea the trip would bless me in return with its warmth and surprising meetings and serene beauty, an unexpected bonus for doing the right thing, and a concept that is ingrained into Amish life. Joy and pleasure, they say, come not from selfish pursuits but as a bonus for obedience to God.

I meet people sometimes who envy the peace and serenity they see among the Amish. So they purchase plain clothing off the Internet and tell me proudly that they just bought a new manual wheat grinder.

My Amish relatives would be the first to insist that they're not perfect, nor is their life a sort of Utopia. And the serenity and contentment on their faces come not from kerosene lanterns or black hats. Rather, they come from the clarity of knowing what's important and what isn't, and then deliberately making choices to live by those priorities. God and their Christian faith come first. New options are evaluated not by whether this would be fun or make money or feel good, but by whether it would be God's will. Faith encompasses all of life.

People are next—primarily family and the local church. Families are large, and the elderly are cared for at home. Personal opinions give way to the larger voice of the church group.

Work is third, serving many purposes—providing for a family, building character, teaching skills to children. Thus, housework is set aside in order to entertain visitors, the efficiency of rubber tractor tires is subject to the church's decision, and the old man reading his Bible is not more holy than his daughters who work hard to care for him.

It would not occur to most Amish to pursue, for their own sake, what many of us consider ends in themselves—fun, entertainment, personal fulfillment, physical fitness, money, influence, creativity. And yet, few of these benefits are missing from their lives, the result of first pursuing what's most important. Fun is sitting under a shade tree with the rest of the family and shelling peas; entertainment is watching two toddlers playing together; staying in shape comes from hoeing the garden and cleaning out the barn; influence and finances from striving for excellence.

Peace and harmony in my own life are not going to come from a vegetable garden and speaking Pennsylvania German. The lingering lesson from this visit to my Amish past is that I need to daily clarify my priorities and actually live by them. Even with my cell phone and store-bought clothes and Kia Optima, I can choose to do that just as thoroughly as my smiling cousin, Katie, in her plain blue dress, climbing into the buggy with her pleasant husband, Harley, and a small package of suspender clips.

Grief and Grace

Carolyn's Miraculous Faith

A hundred different things remind me of my friend Carolyn Schrock's loss, and I have grieved for her in a hundred different ways. Today, again, I thought of her, and of how she was denied a simple reward that every mom ought to enjoy: to have her children grow up to bring her tea and Tylenol when she's sick.

This past week I was knocked off my feet with a vicious virus that began with a sore throat and turned into a strangled cough and what felt like a head full of hot cement. It reminded me of that difficult winter back when my daughter, Emily, was a baby. I seemed to be sick all the time with everything from strep throat to a viral pneumonia. With three small children, I forced myself to keep going, changing diapers and washing little faces in a feverish daze. I remember how desperately I wanted to go to bed, how I thought I would give almost anything to go lie down with a cup of tea.

Parenting at that stage is an act of faith, of giving, investing and sacrificing while believing that someday it will all pay off in mature, generous young adults. It is like planting and watering a garden but waiting many years for the harvest.

How gloriously different my recent sickness was from the old days. Seventeen-year-old Amy made lists of jobs to do around the house and somehow persuaded her little brothers to fall in line and work. Fifteen-year-old Emily did laundry. Both girls brought me pots of tea on pretty little trays, gently closing the bedroom door so I could sleep in peace.

"I've never had this much fun being sick," I croaked, remembering that awful winter 15 years ago and basking in the accomplishment of having turned those dependent babies into young adults with the sympathy and skills to take care of me in return. I was reaping the fruit of my labors, and it was delicious.

And after a hundred ways of grieving for Carolyn, I find a new one today: She had only the investing and giving but was denied the joy of seeing her hard work come to fruition. Her daughters would never be teenagers, bringing her tea when she was sick.

Carolyn was a dark-haired fifth-grader, efficient and hard-working, when I first came to Oregon to teach school. Jeff was the nerdy 14-year-old son of the family I boarded with who discussed electricity and radio waves at the supper table. The two of them married some years later, moved to Washington, and started a family, beginning with three little girls in dark pigtails, and then two boys. I saw them occasionally when they came back to this area to visit.

The phone call came last November with news so shattering, so beyond-words heartbreaking that I couldn't comprehend it: A pickup truck had crossed the median and crashed into the vehicle that Jeff was driving. All five of their children were dead. Jeff was badly injured.

There are no precedents for such grief, no directions through such a jungle of pain. The entire Mennonite community in Oregon wept with them. The city of Spokane, where the accident happened, erupted in gifts, memorials, and sympathetic gas-station readerboards. My friends and I were almost too stunned to function. We called each other on the phone and cried so hard we couldn't talk.

And our faith was tested in ways it had never been tested before.

Faith is easy and seems almost unnecessary when everything is going well, and philosophical arguments on such matters as Calvinism vs. Arminianism seem deep and important. But devastating loss peels away the surface issues and exposes the bare rock: Is there a God? Does he care?

There are, at these times, three theological options: There is no God. There is a God, but he is cold and uncaring. There is a God, and he is loving and involved. None of these options make the grief and pain disappear, but only with the third, we found, could we avoid a dark and utter despair, even if it made no logical sense from our perspective.

The Bible speaks of a mysterious gift called grace, something that makes the weak strong and enables ordinary people to do the impossible. As believers, we are promised that we will not be tested beyond what we can endure, that there will always be enough grace. I have experienced this myself in difficult times, when an unexpected strength held and suspended me above a catastrophe and helped me to do what needed to be done. But surely this was too much. "There can't possibly be enough grace for this," I thought, expecting to hear that Carolyn was curled in a fetal position, sedated and catatonic.

I was wrong. Amazingly, it was Carolyn herself who showed the way for the rest of us. When the police spokeswoman told her there were five fatalities in the accident, she stayed calm and responded, "Thank you for telling me." She made decisions. She helped plan the funeral. She encouraged her husband as he moved from near-death to a long recovery.

And, while others spoke of revenge, lawsuits, and criminal charges, Carolyn was concerned about the driver of the other vehicle, a 55-year-old man named Clifford Helm, who suffered less severe injuries and, according to the Schrock family, did not know why he crossed the median.

Several days after the accident, Carolyn visited Helm in his hospital room. She shook his hand and told him that she and Jeff forgave him. Soon after, he and his family attended the funeral, where five white caskets were placed at the front of the church and 1,500 people came to say goodbye and offer their support.

Six weeks later, Carolyn gave birth to a beautiful, dark-haired daughter, a miracle of new beginnings.

Carolyn, along with her baby and her mother, stopped in at our house recently. "How is it now?" I said, a bumbling way of asking, "Does life go on? Is your soul scarred forever? Is there any beauty in that land of grief in which you now live?"

"There is grace," she said simply, and added, "I feel like Job," referring to the biblical character who lost all his possessions and children in one day, yet did not lose his faith. "He said, 'My ears had heard of you, but now my eyes have seen you.' I feel like I have experienced God for myself instead of just hearing about him." Thoughtfully, she rocked the baby in her carseat, a somewhat worn apparatus with a loose handle that had obviously been used for two or three babies before. She left that day, a woman with her life forever divided into "before" and "after."

I think of her often. I have grieved for her in a hundred ways; she has no doubt grieved in thousands. I have teenage daughters to bring me tea when I'm sick. She lost all her children when the oldest was only 12. And yet, in an amazing and miraculous way, Carolyn continues to lead the rest of us to wholeness and a strong and undiminished faith.

A Journey of Grief

*I*t has been a month of journeys: a sudden trip to the Midwest, a Frodo-like quest, and a pilgrimage into the alien world of grief, with no map or directions and no idea when I would come back home.

On a recent Sunday, I made a list of things to do that week—pick blueberries, weed the garden, and sew pajamas for the boys.

On Monday, my brother, Marcus, phoned at 5:30 a.m. and told me that his 23-year-old son, Leonard, my oldest nephew, had taken his own life the day before. My to-do list and everything else forgotten, I wandered numbly around the house and tried to muster the strength to brew a pot of tea and take a shower while my husband scrambled to find plane tickets and my daughter packed my suitcase.

The next morning, I flew to Minnesota with two of my children, Matt and Emily. It was one of the hardest things we have ever done. In Minneapolis, the three of us would have liked nothing better than to turn and run. Yet we somehow found our way to the rental-car counter and drove west toward the farm.

"We are taking the Ring to the mountain," Matt said, "and it grows heavier the closer we get." All day my feverish, stunned mind had been searching for an analogy, for words to explain what this was like. Then my insightful son provided just what I needed.

He referred, of course, to the *Lord of the Rings*, in which Frodo the Hobbit is chosen to take the One Ring to Mount Doom to throw it back in and destroy it. The closer he gets to the mountain, the heavier the ring becomes. Yet this is Frodo's destiny and his calling, and with the help of his friend, he accomplishes it. That story gave me an odd stability all week. "I am taking the Ring to the mountain," I kept telling myself, before pulling into my brother's driveway, before each visitation, and before the funeral and burial.

It was the longest week of my life. To imagine Leonard's mental suffering was terrible, to see his parents' was much worse—his mother like a little broken sparrow; his dad, with a world of pain in his eyes, gently washing the family van that would bring his son's body home from South Dakota. Since Leonard had lived in South Dakota for the past four years, a visitation was held there before the funeral and burial in Minnesota.

In a surreal side trip, I found myself in a funeral home in a small South Dakota town on a Wednesday evening. As I watched, dozens of clean-cut young cowboys set their black hats on a shelf in the entrance, said a few words to the family, walked respectfully by the casket, then clustered in silence in a small anteroom. Farmers followed them, along with warm, down-home families with pronounced South Dakota accents.

I forced myself to talk to a few people. "How did you know Lenny?" I asked, and out poured their stories. "Lenny took me hunting. I didn't have a big brother, so he said he would be my big brother."

"Lenny was my friend."

"Lenny and I baled hay together."

"Lenny was in my Bible study."

"Lenny was like a son to me."

I thought, over and over, "Oh, Leonard, how could you not know how much you were loved?"

Grieving a suicide means living with a hundred unanswered questions that whine like sirens when I try to sleep. Why would a fun-loving, hardworking young man with truckloads of friends want to die? Were there signs we should have seen? Was there something we should have done? Didn't he know I would have moved heaven and Earth to help him? Why didn't one of his friends knock on the door at the right moment?

Drugs and alcohol are often implicated in suicide, the books say. Leonard used neither. Nor, beyond snowmobiling and bullriding, did he engage in high-risk or self-destructive behavior. But he had admitted, earlier in the year, that he was struggling with depression. Obviously, it was much worse than anyone realized, and I found my anger focusing not on God or Leonard or anyone else but on the thread of depression and mental illness that has afflicted our family tree ever since my great-grandfather took his own life many years ago.

Beyond the questions and the pain, this journey of grief has been full of surprises. The first day's numbness gave way to what seemed like a hot water bottle in my chest, with tubes leading to my eyes. At the oddest times and places, such as the middle of the Denver airport, something punched the water bottle and the tears flowed. At other times, I wanted to cry and couldn't. I had always thought I wouldn't laugh for a month if something like this happened, yet my sister-in-law and I found ourselves laughing hysterically at nothing.

Underneath all the anguish, I was amazed to find something I would never have expected in such a circumstance: a strange, solid sense of peace.

There were touches of grace. The muggy heat gave way to a pleasant breeze on the day of the burial. Emily's 16th birthday fell, unfortunately, on the day before the funeral. Three strangers, friends of my niece, made a special effort to hug Emily and wish her a happy birthday.

Now, we are safely back in the Shire, having taken the Ring to the mountain and shoveled the sandy Minnesota soil into my nephew's grave. I have been sewing pajamas, picking blueberries, and weeding the garden. But the journey continues. I see an advertisement for Western wear in a farm paper, and a rogue wave of grief drenches me. Paul's nephew and his girlfriend sing together at church, I realize I will never attend Leonard's wedding, and the "water bottle" gets a violent punch. When cheerful cashiers say, "How are you?" I flounder for an answer. I am still dazed: Last Sunday, I wore both glasses and contacts to church and wondered why my husband looked so smudged up there in the pulpit.

Touches of grace and surprises continue as well. The most unlikely people say the most comforting words. They tell me they have also taken this journey, and that I will make it—like Frodo—with help from my friends.

"I continue to have a deep sense of peace," my brother says. And so do I. This is surely the biggest surprise of all, a gift to guide us on the long road back home.

Processing the Gifts of Fall

Summer is my favorite season. The sun shines dependably every day, and the air smells of dust from the grass seed harvest, one of the best scents on Earth. Summer is sprinklers, sandals, fuchsias and fresh strawberries. It's cookouts and sleepovers and tea on the porch.

Sometimes I think I'd like it to be summer forever, all warmth and light. No early darkness, no rain, no winter blues to fight, no shivering on cold mornings. Yet the seasons change whether I want them to or not, and each one brings its gifts. Fall's offerings are more subtle than summer's, less visible, more of the soul.

In July, I wake up early as the sun shines through the trees across the creek. Now, I wake to a filtered light through the bedroom window. Fog hides the field across the road, and the oak trees stand out against it in sharp outlines.

A sunny day in September has a charm not found in June. In summer, I expect sunshine. In the fall, I know it could very easily be raining instead. When the light angles onto the front porch and forms a golden square on the floor, I smile like Pigga the cat, who is stretched out in the sun's warmth, happily asleep.

Fall, in many ways, is a time for processing. There are apples and tomatoes to cook and preserve, and there are goals and grief and memories to examine and dissect and put where they belong.

I once took a class in early childhood education in which the instructor introduced me to the idea of what she called "process vs. product." The process of handling a paintbrush and experimenting with colors, she said, is much more important to a child's development than the product of a finished painting; shaping and squeezing clay is more important than a final sculpture. Her theories tickle the back of my mind when I'm processing fruit because, frankly, I hate the process and love the product.

Summer fruits are often picked in gallon buckets and frozen in pint containers—strawberries, blueberries, blackberries. Fall's bounty, in contrast, comes in astonishing quantities—wagons, bushels, tubs, and five-gallon buckets of corn, tomatoes, grapes, and apples. Many Mennonite women love to "put up" fruit and will do a thousand quarts a summer. I, too, love to see dozens of sturdy jars of applesauce lined up in the pantry in military rows, and stacks of plastic bags full of corn in the freezer. But I somehow missed the knack for enjoying the work involved, a mutation in the Mennonite genes, perhaps.

I don't enjoy water dripping off my elbows or having every surface in the kitchen covered with jars, bowls, and kettles. Worms in apples or corn give me chills. Carrying a vat of boiling tomatoes from stove to counter is terrifying, and whenever I pull steaming jars out of a kettle, I fear a stray breeze will shatter them in my hand. Cleanup is the worst part—washing huge canners that don't fit in the sink, chiseling dried bits of corn off the floor, and scrubbing a thousand bits of apple peel out of the Victorio-strainer screen. Yet there is really no way around the work, no Candy-Land slides to whisk us from boxes of apples to jars of fresh sauce.

I try to see the value of the process, however tedious and messy it may be: Paul and the children sitting in a circle in the yard, husking corn. Amy and Emily cutting apples and talking girl stuff. Seeing a box of fruit become dessert for my family in January. Teaching the children that food does not show up in a can at WinCo through some kind of spontaneous generation.

Produce is not the only thing that is washed, cut, and preserved at this time of year. My favorite gift of this season is its gentler, quieter pace and the chance to process matters of the heart. This is nearly impossible in summer, which, at our place, is noisy and constantly busy. Sprinklers tick in the garden, creek-wet children hang their towels on the porch rail and run upstairs to change, Jenny leaves her paints and crayons all over the table, balls and other objects fly through the air, and the younger children have loud arguments on, for example, whether or not Emily was winking with both eyes at the same time. Paul, preoccupied with harvest, pops in the back door at odd times, shouting on his cell phone about seed samples and lot numbers.

In autumn, life slows down, beginning with the flies. In summer, houseflies dart in when the kitchen door opens and spring out of reach when I sneak up with the fly swatter. But every September, for reasons I have never understood, the flies migrate to the living room and fly in slow loops at the center of the room while I flail with the flyswatter like a badminton player gone mad. Unaffected, they fly lazily on. The flies, it seems, signal the rest of life to slow its pace as well. When the children disappeared out the door on the day after Labor Day, I was handed a gift of solitude.

This year, for the first time, everyone in the family but me is in school full time. Paul has returned to teaching all day,

Matt and Amy are in college, the younger ones attend our church school. In this blessing of uninterrupted time, I list my goals for the next year, read the waiting stack of books, and work on writing and sewing projects. And I grieve.

My 23-year-old nephew's suicide a few months earlier was a shattering experience for us all. In the weeks that followed, I found that I had almost no tolerance for the normal distractions and noise of family life. So the solitude that fall brought has been a gift, a chance to work through this loss, to dissect and stir and examine. I can pray, go on a bike ride, or sit on the porch swing and cry.

I sometimes wish I could skip the process of grief and jump to the final product of healing and greater maturity and compassion. Yet I know that without deliberately going through this pain, washing and cutting and stirring, I will never move beyond it.

"To everything," the Bible says in Ecclesiastes, "there is a season, and a time to every purpose under the heaven ... A time to plant, and a time to pluck up that which is planted ... A time to weep, and a time to laugh; a time to mourn, and a time to dance."

The gifts of fall are precious and the work they bring is difficult, but I believe I will come to agree with the biblical writer who concluded, after writing of harvest and work and tears and laughter, "He hath made everything beautiful in his time."

Connecting to
the Amish

The school shooting in Pennsylvania in October 2006 pushed the Amish community reluctantly on stage before the entire world. Their loss overwhelmed us, their strength and forgiveness astounded us, and their lifestyle fascinated us more than ever.

"Who are they, really?" people wondered. "Are they like us?" "Is their pain as intense as ours would be?" "Do they want the sympathy we long to extend?"

For me, the most haunting part of the tragedy was the little 7- and 8-year-old sisters who were killed. When my sister, Becky, and I were that age, we were, like them, little Amish girls in an Amish school. The thought of a man coming into our school with both sexual abuse and murder on his mind is incomprehensible. We would have had no concept of such things, no context, no words, no compartment in our little worlds for such evil.

My oldest brother, I was told, heard the news and wept, thinking of his little sisters at that age, with their big innocent brown eyes.

We were Amish before Amish was cool, back when my brother's teacher in public school referred to him derisively as "Dutchy." That was before one could buy dreamy paintings of little Amish girls with kittens in their laps, and long before insurance companies and wineries in Lancaster County painted pictures of buggies on their signs.

My own response to the shootings was to plunge unexpectedly into a sea of Amish memories. I remembered details I hadn't thought of in years, such as how the buggy wheels rasped on the road, how the sound of the horse's hooves changed to a steady clip-clop when we turned off a gravel road onto pavement, and how the sounds seemed to amplify inside the stiff navy-blue bonnet I wore over my white organdy cap. I remembered being in one of a long line of buggies, and how Becky and I giggled when the horse behind us seemed to be peering into the little window in the back of the buggy. I recalled Pennsylvania-German words I thought I had forgotten: *die Laut*, the casket, *die Engel*, the angels.

Especially, I remembered details of my grandparents' funerals—first the wake, when the body lay in a bedroom, which didn't seem repugnant at all, and we all sat on benches and sang for hours while people came to pay their respects. Then, the funeral, when an astonishing number of people sat on backless benches all over the house and the preaching went on and on. People filed by the casket at the end of the service—they came and came and came, men in black suits, women in black dresses. I knew they had all been in the house somewhere, but where? We joined the procession to the country cemetery and, at Grandma Miller's burial, a group of perhaps 10 young people sang a song about *die Engel* while the girls' black shawls flapped in the cold wind.

My parents' leaving of the Old Order and joining the "Beachy" Amish (named for a leader, Moses Beachy), was a gradual process. They didn't want us involved in the self-destructive activities that many Old Order Amish young people engaged in during their *rumspringa* (running around) years before they joined the church.

So by the time I was 10 years old, we had a car, electricity, and a phone, although we still wore plain solid-color dresses and white caps. Few of our Amish relatives condemned us for leaving, recognizing that faith in God mattered more than buggies or cars.

It seems the more our society has moved away from the Amish values of farming, family, simplicity, and community, the more the Amish lifestyle has been idealized, leading to best-selling Beverly Lewis novels about the Amish, and cross-stitch patterns of little boys in broad black hats. When my computer refuses to cooperate, or when I run into Amish relatives at family events, I sometimes have a strange longing to be part of that world again. It looks simple, warm, and defined.

But the truth is that I could never belong again; that door has closed. This, perhaps, is part of the Amish appeal — knowing that even though we can stand at the gate and look wistfully inside, we can never be part of that world. I sometimes meet people who try. The women wear long, full dresses, the men beards and big hats. "We're becoming Amish," they say, and brag about their new treadle sewing machine. How do I tell them that they have a hundred details wrong, from the wrinkled cap to the much-too-confident look on their faces? Worse, they do it alone, when the very essence of Amish life is community.

As a Beachy Amish teenager, I tried to define our lives for my Lutheran friends. "We're just people like everyone else," I would say, mystified at their curiosity. A Granny Smith apple tastes the same to an Amishman as to anyone else. Amish eyes become farsighted after age 40, a ham in the oven smells the same, a stubbed toe hurts equally.

And yet, it is equally true that the Amish are very different. For us, there was first of all a language barrier. English was for the world out there, formal and stilted. Pennsylvania German, or "Dutch" as we called it, was for home and warmth and belonging. We went to the door and spoke English to the salesman on the porch, then shut the door and reverted to Dutch, laughing, recounting the conversation with, perhaps, a snide comment about the salesman's persistence.

There was usually a distinct sense of us and them. "They" talked about sports and TV shows and getting their hair done, things we knew little about. One put on a proper face for public, where people were often patronizing, reverent, curious, or at times hostile. At home, the formality dropped and we ran around barefooted and laughed and had water fights. Looking at news photos of a long line of buggies driving past aggressive photographers, I thought again of this dichotomy. Essentially, at heart, the two groups of people were the same. And yet, at the same time, they were completely different in language, goals, employment, recreation, clothing, and much more.

I saw this stark difference when my Grandma Yoder died 18 years ago. After the funeral, we ate at my cousin Edna's house. It was packed with hundreds of people standing shoulder to shoulder, all of them dressed in black. For three hours, a line of people inched down to the basement for the meal; a similar line inched its way back up. My sisters and I had a wonderful time catching up with relatives, but the day was less enjoyable for our husbands, who escaped outside and sat in the van, and who felt, as many Americans probably would, that they had almost nothing in common with these people.

A tragedy such as the Amish school shooting in Pennsylvania, makes us reach across our differences and seek for connections. Perhaps we are trying to justify our deep feelings or prove that our grief is valid, and so we grope for points of contact. In this case, those of us with Amish in our background or distant relatives among the bereaved felt compelled to tell everyone. Every mother of young children saw her daughters lined up along that blackboard, her sons forced to leave their sisters behind.

On a Lancaster Online page of condolences, people from around the world shared their slightest connections to the Amish. "The Amish Community is very special to us," wrote one. "We have visited many times and always come away with peaceful hearts." On the Internet, bloggers recalled how they once drove through Lancaster County and waved at little Amish children on scooters on their way to school.

The truth is, at a time like this, there is no need to prove a connection. Nothing unites us in a common humanity like a child's death. It's not "us" modern people and "them" folks in their buggies; it's all "us," Amish, Muslim, Catholic, or anything else. Losing a child is losing a child, and we are all justified in reading the news and weeping.

As John Donne wrote, "No man is an island, entire of itself; every man is a piece of the continent; a part of the main. ... Any man's death diminishes me, because I am involved in mankind; and therefore never send to know for whom the bell tolls; it tolls for thee."

Pruning's Purpose

No one has ever taught me to properly prune the grapevines south of the house, so I always cut enthusiastically and hope for the best, which has never seemed to bother the vines. Each year they send 15-foot tendrils all over the arbor and even far up into the nearby pine trees, and then produce a solid crop of grapes.

This year's pruning began on a rare pleasant day in February, inspired less by the grapevine's needs than by the emerging flock of daffodils on the ground below—I wanted to enjoy their yellow beauty without the interference of a tangle of drooping vines. When I finished, the discarded vines lay on the grass and the arbor and daffodils made a neat, uncluttered picture in the yard.

Cleaning out the oak grove was a much bigger project.

My brother-in-law, Kenneth, owns the fescue field north of our house and also the band of oak trees just across the road. Until recently, the trees stood knee-deep in a tangled undergrowth of blackberries and saplings and unnamed bushes. Then Kenneth and a few friends moved in with a chainsaw and heavy equipment. I watched, worried that the entire site was being turned into more fescue field. But when all the branches and brambles were cleared away, the oak trees remained, clean and clearly outlined, from exposed roots on the ground to long crooked branches against the sky.

These pruning endeavors were soon followed, coincidentally, by a Sunday school lesson from the Gospel of John that likens Jesus to the main grapevine and we followers to the branches. God is the gardener who prunes the vines to make them more fruitful, the verses say, implying that God is not an indiscriminate whacker like me but knows exactly where to cut, and when. Such trimming also implies suffering, that worrisome experience we all try to avoid, from inconvenience and irritations to debilitating pain and loss.

Trusting that there is a gardener and that he knows what he is doing is a fine theory, easily assented to in a theoretical Sunday school discussion, or when the cuts are not too painful and it seems they might actually be for some purpose. I think, for example, of our 18-year-old daughter, Amy, who recently returned home after six weeks away and found that she is now shorter than all but one of her five siblings. She has no hope of ever being taller, which is not a huge handicap, to be sure, and yet she has had to accept that people will never take her seriously at first glance and she will never be able to reach top cupboards unassisted by stepstools.

Yet it is not too hard to believe that there may be something redemptive in this. "Aunt Amy" will no doubt be known to all her nieces and nephews as the first adult thcy equal in height when they hit their growth spurt. Perhaps she will be able to influence them at eye level in a way that larger adults cannot.

But there are also times when it is much harder to believe in a divine purpose, when the cutting is done with chainsaws instead of shears, and the underbrush is cleared out ruthlessly with heavy equipment.

My niece, Annette, flew out from Pennsylvania recently to spend a week with us. A beautiful 27-year-old, she is in many ways defined by the losses in her life. Other young couples, she says wistfully, seem to float through their first years of marriage with only a wave or two of financial struggles or in-law issues rocking their boat. In contrast, Annette and her husband, Jay, have faced storms far worse than any of their friends have experienced.

Four days after they were engaged to be married, Annette had surgery on a detached retina in her eye. She recovered at her future in-laws' house, and Jay had his first taste of what "In sickness and health" involved when Annette reacted violently to her medication. Her face was swollen and oozing and discolored, and she kept throwing up over and over. Unfazed, Jay took care of her, confirming that she had indeed chosen the right man.

Her eye has continued to be troublesome, both with medical bills and complications that limit her life in unexpected ways. Eyestrain keeps her from doing much work on the computer or reading newspapers, and she worries about how a future pregnancy might be affected by the powerful medications she has to take.

If Annette's eye was a sneaker wave upsetting their lives, her brother's suicide the following summer was a tsunami that changed the entire landscape. Annette was three years older than Leonard and, despite the two of them being very close, she had no idea this tragedy was coming. Then, six weeks after Leonard's death, their only sister was in the hospital having a just-in-time appendectomy.

Annette came to Oregon in search of some "aunt time," as she put it. The two of us sat at the kitchen table for hours, stirring our coffee and talking about changes and grief and loss. She talked about what she calls "The Journey." It encompasses the months past and the years yet to come—the cutting, the growing, the endless questions. If she had called Leonard the night before, would things have turned out differently? If she had been first on the scene, would she have seen a clue the investigators missed?

I longed to do the impossible and dispense answers that would make everything make sense. But she was adamant: She doesn't need pat religious-formula answers, nor does she want to be told that life is all random and there is no purpose or hope. What she needs is people to come alongside her in the journey, to acknowledge her daily struggle, to support her, to listen, to hear the hard questions, to give her time to find the answers herself.

Our conversation wandered to people we know who have been transformed by suffering, changed from cold and somewhat judgmental to warm and empathetic. "Was there no other way to do this?" we asked each other. "Did it have to take that?" And, a dangerous question: "Are we supposed to think it was actually better this way, that it was worth the sacrifice?" Annette is honest about her struggles with faith. She told of how she went to get groceries the night her sister was in the hospital. "Oh, I was so mad," she said. "I stomped around that grocery store and I kept thinking, 'Can I trust you, God? Can I really trust you? With my family? With anything?'"

Then she laughed and continued. "This is Lancaster County, Pennsylvania, you know, and they play hymns on my grocery-store's PA system. And while I was stomping around pushing that grocery cart, the song 'All to Jesus I Surrender' started playing. I said, 'OK, God, I get the message.'" I chuckled with her, imagining the scene and relieved to see that for all the difficulty in her life, her quirky sense of humor remains.

Actually, I can tell that, like the oak trees across the road, the person Annette really is has been outlined and clarified more clearly than ever before. She has always been funny, loving, strong, and wise; she still is. "I make it," she said, "by the grace of God and my stubborn will."

For all the things I do not know, I do know this: What remains after the pruning is firm and solid, spring will eventually come, and new growth will appear, determined and green.

Finding the Howevers

We sat at the kitchen table last week, my 17-year-old daughter, Emily, and I, discussing how someone who missed almost her entire senior year of high school could write a graduation speech. "There's nothing to say," she insisted.

And I said, "Pretend I don't know a thing, and tell me what you've been through." So she talked and I took notes, and when she finished telling about the complicated anguish of being sick for so long, she stopped.

"However..." I prodded, like a too-typical, kiss-it-and-make-it-all-better mom.

"There are no howevers!" she burst out. "I feel like everybody will expect me to say, 'However, all these wonderful character-building things came out of this so it was all worthwhile and now I'm so patient and compassionate and everything.' But in my mind there are no howevers yet! I still feel sick, and I don't think I've changed into some sort of wonderful patient person. And I don't understand why I had to go through this!"

"Then say exactly that," I said, and she did, the following Thursday, in her new elfin-silver dress with the green jacket, and in the audience people who love her listened and wiped their eyes.

Emily has had vague health issues for years—food allergies and migraine headaches and prolonged bouts of the flu. But by the time she was 16 she seemed to have outgrown much of this and reveled in the activities of a normal junior year of high school. She had endless plans for her senior year. "I was going to be editor of the yearbook," she said, "and I was all excited about making it interesting and unique. I wanted to get a job on the side and take college algebra at a community college, because this was the first year I could drive myself around. And I was going to write and direct a play for the youth group to act out for a fundraiser."

A week into the school year she got sick.

"No big deal," we thought, and after a week she was better again. But the aches and fever returned, and by October she was constantly ill and had been examined, tested, poked, and re-examined, and the medical experts seemed to have no more answers than we did.

I Googled "teenager fever aches fatigue" and wanted to throw the mouse at the computer and run screaming from the room as an ominous list popped up, from leukemia on down through mononucleosis and fibromyalgia. Only one test result was positive and that only slightly: West Nile Fever, a virus spread by mosquitoes. One doctor said, "No, it's not West Nile"; another said, "Yes, of course it is." We chose to believe that it was, a conclusion affirmed by other victims whose experiences paralleled Emily's. There is no cure, we were told, and recovery can take from two weeks to two years.

In her speech, Emily described the moment when she realized she would probably be sick for a long time. "I sat in the darkness and cried, thinking about all my wonderful plans. I had to finally accept the fact that I wouldn't be able to do them."

"Surely by Thanksgiving she'll be well," we said in the fall. "Well, then, surely by Christmas, by spring, by summer."

By January, she was so weak she asked me to buy her a cane.

I have learned that for every sick child there is a caregiver parent in the background, enduring not fevers and aches and accumulating losses, but the quiet grief of watching. When she asked for a cane I thought, "OK, this is it, end of the road, I cannot buy my beautiful, elegant, 17-year-old a cane." But of course I did anyhow, because that is what parents do.

The sickness had not destroyed Emily's sense of fun, an important "however." She decorated the cane with stickers and pink ribbons, and named it John McCane. As she felt able, which wasn't often, Emily did her schoolwork at home. Mercifully, the school board of our small church school told her she could go ahead with graduation exercises, and her principal dad promised to make sure she eventually finished the required courses so she could get her diploma.

With characteristic honesty, Emily described how the sickness tested her faith. "I always believed before this sickness came that God would never give me more than I could handle. But I realized during this time that the big flaw in that is we can handle anything if we're not given a choice. We think there are things we can't handle ... we'd just go crazy ... but if something is handed to you, you just get through it if you think you can or not, because going crazy is a lot harder than it sounds. I can't say I ever got mad at God, or that I ever felt like he deserted me, I just don't understand so many things."

And then she told the audience that they are no doubt waiting for her to list the "howevers," but that there are no howevers yet. She ended the speech with gratitude to everyone who had been there for her during this time, and added,

"My mom has done the most of everyone. I have been sick for nine months, and she still brings me tea in bed. I cannot thank her enough."

Listening teary-eyed to this tribute, I had to disagree with Emily. I think there are many howevers in her story, like seedlings pushing out of the dark garden soil, unseen at first glance and then suddenly there, all in a line, tiny and green. She just can't see them yet—the grace, the growth, the hidden gifts of empathy and gratitude. Emily still doesn't feel well, but she is strong enough that John McCane hangs unused behind her bedroom door.

She has new determination, goals, and creativity, gradually redecorating her brother's old bedroom for herself in an eye-popping "Shimmering Lime" color and asking for a dress form for a graduation gift so she can design clothes and costumes. "She will not be the same Emily coming out of this as she was going into it," a wise friend told me.

I would not for a second calculate whether the hard times have been worth the howevers, but I do know that I like the emerging Emily, this newly mature young woman who waters my life with laughter dipped from sickness and gentleness wrung from suffering.

Sloshing Emotions and New Pursuits

*L*ately I seem to be crying more than normal, not because of depression or trauma, but because I am a sentimental 40-something mom brimful of liquid emotions that easily slosh over the edge. Especially at Christmas, with its music and celebration and family times, a slight jar brings the tissues out of my pocket.

So I cried happily when my two handsome teenage sons sang in their choir's Christmas concert, Ben's newly deep voice vibrating out confidently on the bass notes of the jubilant, "All the Trees of the Field Shall Clap Their Hands." This child spent too much of his life thinking he hated to sing, and yet there he was, miraculously singing out and enjoying it—and what could I do but cry?

My brother sent me a picture of his family, with everyone cheerfully smiling. But I looked at it and wept at what was missing—my nephew who died tragically a year and a half ago.

We went to hear the African Children's Choir in Harrisburg one evening. Bright-eyed little children the age of my youngest daughter took the microphone and introduced themselves as Joshua or Esther or Enoch and said they want to be a pilot or nurse or plumber when they grew up.

And then I thought about Kenya going up in flames after the recent election, and innocent people suffering even more, and our son Steven coming from that life to this one, and it all bubbled out in hot tears. "Tears are significant," our Kenyan friend, Vincent, told me once. "It shows you a lot about a person's character, what they cry about."

So, I wonder, what does it say about me when I get the most emotional of all about my children leaving home? At our large Smucker family Christmas, someone asked me how I was doing, and I unexpectedly burst into tears because, I sputtered, I have all these conflicting feelings about my kids growing up.

Matt, our oldest, finished his finals at Oregon State University in early December and came home for a month, and then Amy flew in from South Carolina for the holidays. I felt and behaved like a contented, clucking hen with all her chicks safely back in the nest. The feeling of utter fulfillment I got from having everyone home, especially when we lingered around the supper table for long, rambling discussions, was just what I had hoped for and expected.

What took me by surprise was the paradox of feeling such joy yet at the same time being plagued by a vague hunger, a longing for something from my children that I could not define and that they seemed unable to give. Both Matt and Amy enjoyed being at home, high-fiving wildly while listening to Ducks games in the boys' bedroom, opening gifts on Christmas morning, and cleaning the kitchen together. But they seemed equally eager to dash off to hang out with their friends or go shopping or take in a church youth activity. I found myself watching them go, perplexed by this strange, dissatisfied wanting.

My husband's sister, Lois, whose three oldest, as she says, "are marrying faster than they came," had this explanation after my little meltdown at the family gathering: "You want them to need you like they used to," she told me sympathetically. "It's this paradox," she went on, "you've worked for this all their lives, to get them to where they can make it on their own, and then when they do, you want them to need you again just like they did when they were little, and they don't, and it hurts."

The more I thought about this, the more sense it made, especially since I had chosen to invest more of my life into my children than in any other pursuit. It also made me suddenly understand my mom a lot better. So many times I have gone home and spent time with her, yet when I left I felt like there was a vague disappointment in her soul that I could not fix, a hunger I could not satisfy.

"Sometimes I wish I just had one day with all of you little again," she would say wistfully. "Just one day, all at home and around me again."

Why? I wondered at the time. As poor as we were then, as hard as she had to work, as difficult as I was, why would she want to go back?

Now, I'm starting to understand.

When three of us siblings all left home in a single summer, Mom coped not with my sort of dripping waterworks but by throwing herself into a frenzy of quilting and crafts. In the following years she produced quilts, pillows, dolls, rugs, and much more, coming out on the other side of that transition with polished skills and a large, colorful collection of useful artwork.

A gentle inner nudging has been telling me that, busy as I am, I should do a bit of the same. In fact, I turned impulsively to my 17-year-old daughter, Emily, the other day and announced, "I think God might be telling me to make a quilt instead of obsessing about my kids." She looked a bit stunned and then said, in teenage lingo, "Well! That was random!"

Thankfully Emily, like the rest of the family, is kind and indulgent with me, recognizing that this is not an easy transition, and tolerating my tears and outbursts with gentle amusement.

Then came a sweet little confirmation that quilting was the right pursuit. On the very day that I had told Emily I was thinking I should make a quilt, Lois pulled her sisters-in-law together at our family supper and announced, "I've decided that for your Christmas gift I'm going to pay for all of us to take a quilting class together. Depending on which class we decide to take, and if we do our homework, we can all have a king-sized quilt pieced by the end."

Surprisingly, for all my delight and gratitude at this news, I didn't cry. I just knew, deep down, that someone was watching out for me, life would go on, I was going to find new worlds to conquer, and everything was actually, eventually going to be all right.

Gathering In

Swatting Flies
Like Grandma

Fall is the season of crane flies, skinny awkward insects that my 17-year-old daughter, Emily, describes as "a little bit like an overgrown mosquito and a little bit like a daddy-long-legs with wings." The lights on the porch attract most of the crane flies around here, but a few slipped inside one evening, resting delicately on the kitchen walls. Emily, who hates bugs, couldn't leave them alone. She rolled up a newspaper and went to battle.

Watching her, I had a sudden memory of my mom, in recent summers, and my grandma, many years ago, marching around the kitchen with a flyswatter in hand and murderous determination in their eyes. These were kind-hearted women who crooned in German to newborn piglets and spoiled the cats, but they had no patience with flies in the kitchen. After she killed one, my grandma often told us, in her German dialect, "Every time you 'schwat' a fly, seven more come to the funeral."

As I watched Emily stalk the crane flies I thought to myself, "OK, this will be the big test: If she leaps up on a chair to reach a crane fly, I will know for sure that she is officially carrying the torch of her grandma and great-grandma." Sure enough, Emily boosted herself onto a green stool in the corner and smacked a bug high on the wall, then jumped down, looking satisfied, and took off after the next one.

Seeing this remarkable similarity to Emily's foremothers made me wonder again about the intricate threads that bind generations of women. How much are we tied into family patterns without even knowing it, and how much power do we have to carry on the good and meaningful and to break free from the unhealthy and unhappy?

When Emily and her older sister, Amy, were little, we lived in a cabin in Canada and I heated water on the stove for their baths. As I bathed them in the galvanized-tin bathtub, I imagined us as part of a long chain of mothers and daughters—my mom scrubbing me like this in the little house in Kalona, Iowa; Mom's mother washing her in a farmhouse in Indiana; and my great-grandma, "Mommie Schlabach," washing Grandma in a makeshift tub wherever their family had most recently moved. And I wondered: Did each generation before me have the hopes for their daughters that I had for mine?

I come from a long line of strong, determined women. Deep in the Amish subculture, the ebbs and flows of the women's movement in the larger society completely passed them by. They never got the message that housewives should be all dainty in lipstick and heels, or the later one that they should be liberated and find fulfillment through employment or education or positions of power.

Instead, these women raised large families and hoed their huge gardens and sold produce in town. They hitched up the temperamental horse to the wagon and picked huckleberries in the back 40 all day and then came home to do a day's worth of housework in the evening. They built closets in the bedrooms and sewed denim trousers for the men and chopped the chickens' heads off on butchering days.

And they seemed to love every minute of it.

"We wouldn't have had to work so hard," my Aunt Vina told me once, chuckling, "but I guess we used to think we were half horse."

I am in many ways as traditional as my great-grand-mother. I like children, stories, cats, making something out of nothing, and growing a vegetable garden. Somehow, though, I missed out on the endless energy of previous generations, and I envy their stamina and courage.

I can think of only one area where I actually try to be different, and that is in the hidden thread of silence that connects these women. They had plenty to say on almost every subject, but there were times and situations when they should have spoken, and, for reasons I don't fully understand, did not. My great-grandmother had a child at the age of 15, and I am told that she did not talk about this. In later generations, there was abuse that no one exposed, and an unwillingness to ask for badly needed help or to talk about personal things, or even to verbally express affection.

My mother, in her own way, was determined to be different. When I was a child, she courageously told us what her mother had been unable to tell her—the things we needed to know when our bodies started changing.

While my great-grandmother's silence seems incomprehensible to me—and I am far more likely than my mom to call a friend when I have a bad day—it still has not been easy to find and speak the words for both affection and anger, to ask for help when I need it, to speak out, to realize that secrets lose their power when exposed to light. For all the mistakes we and our mothers made, we keep believing that our daughters will somehow get it all right, that they will keep the healthy and humorous legacies in one hand while releasing the regrettable and sad with the other.

I see this in Jenny, my fearless, red-headed 8-year-old, who likes to climb and jump and play kickball with the boys. "It makes me feel tough when I'm all banged up," she told me the other day, proudly examining the bruises on her shins. Another day she announced, "It makes me feel so good when people cheer for me. Like when I'm playing soccer and Kyle says, 'Go Jenny!'" Jenny's energy and determination come straight from her grandmothers, I'm convinced, and that makes me smile. But what really makes me happy is to see how easily she identifies both her feelings and the words to express them, freely and confidently.

I am immensely proud of my daughters and wish only good things for them. Realistically, though, I know that they will make their own choices and their own mistakes. But when I see them roll up a newspaper and stalk through the kitchen with a determined glint in their eyes, I am confident of this: They come from good stock, and it would take an awful lot to defeat them.

Pondering in My Heart

I memorized the Christmas story in the first grade, in preparation for the program at our little Amish school. I still have the dress I wore that night, a maroon corduroy dress with a pocket on the front, that Mom had sewn for me.

As I recall, the dress was much more exciting to me than the lines I recited. We younger ones quoted from the second chapter of Luke, with its descriptions of startled shepherds and rejoicing angels. The older children repeated prophecies from the Old Testament, rattling through "Behold, a virgin shall conceive, and bear a son, and shall call his name Immanuel," and stumbling over "But thou, Bethlehem Ephratah, though thou be little among the thousands of Judah, yet out of thee shall he come forth unto me that is to be ruler in Israel."

By the time I was an adult I could recite large swaths of the Christmas scriptures and had heard and read the story of Christ's birth hundreds of times, a familiarity that unfortunately dulled the wonder of the essential kernel at the heart of it all: Jesus coming as a baby in a poor family to rescue a lost world. I always believed the story, and loved it, but I remember the moment when it actually became real to me, bursting out of the familiar poetic narrative like a sudden bright light from a dark window.

Paul and I had been married for nearly a year and a half, and we were consumed with the wondrous fact that we were going to have a child. I had survived months of relentless nausea and was just getting back on my feet when a friend invited me to see the Christmas pageant in Rickreall with her. Rickreall is a small town north of Corvallis that has put on an elaborate dramatization of the Christmas story for more than 60 years. All dialogue and narration are strictly quotations from the Bible, but the actors include plenty of dramatic fill-ins and pantomime. A large choir sings between scenes.

I sat there enthralled as a richly costumed angel brought good news and the choir sang like the original heavenly chorus. Then a live donkey emerged from the side of the stage, and a young woman, playing Mary, sat on his back. Mary looked tired, and her hand rested on a gentle bulge on her stomach. That was when it struck me, and I wept at the astounding realization: Mary was... why she actually was... *pregnant*! Pregnant with her first child like I was with mine, full of the same newness and wonder, facing the same enormous changes and fears. I did not analyze our differences then, such as the prospect of laying her baby in a manger vs. a clean bassinet at the Silverton Hospital. I only saw with astonishing clarity that Mary was not just a sweet character in a familiar story. She had been a real woman with a real pregnancy.

In the classic children's book, *The Best Christmas Pageant Ever*, the narrator says of Imogene Herdman, the wild, uncombed girl who usurped the role of Mary in the Sunday school play: "Christmas just came over her all at once, like a case of chills and fever. And so she was crying, and walking into the furniture." As it did for Imogene, Christmas came over me all at once at that old-fashioned pageant in Rickreall.

I am older now, and while I chuckle at the hyper-sensitive emotions that accompanied that first pregnancy, I still find Christmas coming over me, cutting through 40 years of repetition to become glowing and vivid. Some years it hits me when I hear "Silent Night" playing above overdone decorations in a crowded department store, sometimes in the music of *The Messiah*, sometimes in my own children, innocent in new homemade dresses or awkward costumes, reciting Luke 2 in a school Christmas program.

This year, I find myself drawn once again to Mary, her life, her motherhood. An obscure little phrase jumps out of the story and stays in my mind as I wrap gifts and prepare shepherd robes. We are told that as Mary became aware of her son's purpose, through shepherds showing up unexpectedly and an old man's sudden mysterious blessing, she "marvelled at those things." And she "kept all these things, and pondered them in her heart."

It seems, in a way, an odd response to the drama of rich strangers bringing frankincense or a special star in the sky. Why didn't she tell all her friends or broadcast it to the neighborhood? Instead, she pondered.

I think of this phrase because I am in a pondering season myself as I observe my three young-adult children. I am not much like Mary and my children's destiny is not like Jesus', yet I find myself watching and marvelling as their own callings unfold.

I've had my years of talking to them, repeating phrases that I picture engraved on permanent cassette tapes in their heads, whirring to life when needed. "Think about how your behavior affects other people." "Don't interrupt." And "Eat what is set before you with a thankful heart," which I always insisted was in the Bible somewhere, but I couldn't find it just then. (My oldest son, Matt, told me recently that, as a modern young man, the phrases in his head are actually on CDs instead of cassettes. But, he assured me, they are there all the same.)

But now, it's time to be quiet.

Two children have left the nest, one to a job in South Carolina and one to college in Corvallis. This year, for the first time, I am in the role of having someone come home to me for Christmas. I am the one fluttering and feathering, putting clean sheets on the beds, jotting down their favorite foods.

And, like Mary, I watch, pray, and wonder.

Is Amy fitting in? Is she happy? Matt is having a hard time with his first engineering classes and has wondered at times if this is really the right major for him. I wish I could tell him what to do, but I can't. And how, I wonder, can Emily best channel her unusual talents after she graduates from high school?

When my big kids are together, they speak in code, exchanging looks or short phrases that communicate in a language I don't know. I sense that they tell each other things and then add, "Don't tell Mom," just like my sister used to tell me when she had to drive through gang territory to commute to her new job in Los Angeles.

But I also sense that this is the time to listen and love and ponder and cook more food, but not to talk. I rest in the fact that, as Jesus' calling unfolded with time, so will theirs. So Christmas has come over me gently this year. I read the familiar story and know that for all the mysteries and unknowns in our family's lives, the goodwill is toward all of us, and ours is again the wonder and hope and joy.

Apple Dumplings

*O*ur neighbor, Leroy, who is my husband Paul's second cousin if you go through Paul's grandma, and his half-first cousin once removed if you route it through his grandpa, gives us apples every year that he grows on land that once belonged to my husband's grandpa, Orval.

The apples are wonderful and the eight of us eat them recklessly, but even then I noticed last week that they were starting to get a bit dried and wrinkled. Since my mother taught me thoroughly that throwing away food was one of the worst sins, I determined to use up these apples rather then toss them on the compost pile. I regularly make apple crisp and sometimes pies, but I wanted to try something I vaguely remembered Mom making. It involved dough wrapped around apple halves, with a bit of syrup at the bottom of the pan.

I hunted through a cookbook from a neighboring church, knowing that church cookbooks have the best tried-and-true recipes anywhere, and there I found what I wanted: apple dumplings. And the contributor was Elsie Knox.

As I mixed up the dough, I thought about heritage and generations and life coming full circle. Twenty-two years ago I married into a large, noisy, generous, opinionated clan whose genealogy was forever complicated by the fact that two of the patriarchs had married their stepfather's younger sisters, giving the family tree a violent twist that we are still untangling today.

Paul and I spent eight years in mission work in northwestern Ontario, far from his Oregon roots. Then, twelve years ago, we moved back to this area and immersed our children in the joys of playing in the creek with cousins, large Christmas dinners with the extended family, and Grandma stopping by with a loaf of fresh cracked-wheat bread.

We live in a 95-year-old farmhouse that was built in 1911 by my husband's great-grandfather. He and his wife raised 10 children here, then the house passed on to my husband's half-great-aunt—well, if you figure it that way. The other way she was his first cousin once removed. And her name was Elsie Knox, the contributor of the apple dumpling recipe.

So it is a strange thing to be making Elsie's recipe to feed my six children in the same kitchen in which Elsie no doubt made the same recipe to feed her six. Only hers were all boys, and they grew up to become the Knox Brothers, a singing group familiar to many Southern Gospel music fans.

There are those who are called to live far from their families and roots. The day will no doubt come for our children when they will move from this comfortable nest to a place where faces are unfamiliar and all the apples are tasteless and store-bought.

So now, while I still have the opportunity, I bake dumplings from a family recipe with apples from a generous neighbor, filling my children with solid roots and values to give them strength for whatever their futures hold.

Blackberries for an Addled Mind

I wonder sometimes why blackberries ripen at the time of year when I am least able to enjoy them. I would prefer them six months later, in February, a juicy boost in the middle of winter when I could make a daily pilgrimage to the berry patch. Instead, the wild blackberries around here ripen at the end of August, right at the time when the demands and obligations of late summer seem overwhelming.

In July, I just manage to stay on top of the weeding, watering, schedules, canning, cooking, and social activities. But by the last week or two of August the flowerbeds are drying up, the weeds on the far end of the garden are out of control, and the green beans should have been picked yesterday. All the windows look dusty and cobwebby, the dog is scratching miserably, Gravenstein apples are dropping off the tree, and the boys still need school clothes—a job I put off as long as possible in hopes that the new jeans won't be outgrown before the first report cards come home.

Some moms I know respond by cutting their losses with the petunias and pinning their hopes for relief on the first day of school and the fall rains. I respond by questioning my sanity, first with an exasperated, "What was I thinking—to plant all these beans and say I'd help with Bible Memory Camp?" but mostly because of the disconcerting evidence that my brain has stopped working. I am absentminded at the best of times, but late summer is when I stand lost and confused in the middle of the WinCo parking lot trying to locate my car—or wait, did I drive the van today?—right after I fed a cartful of sticky pop cans into the machine, forgot to redeem the refund coupon, forgot to return the important phone call, and left my clipboard with all my careful lists lying on the counter at OfficeMax.

I get to the middle of a sentence and forget where I began and where I was going. Normally, I at least make it close to the end of the sentence before I do this. I yell at the dog to quit barking at the sheep, but I call him Steven instead of Hansie.

My seed-sacking nephew, Zack, I was told, texted his mom one day and said, "Is Aunt Dorcas OK? She seems kind of spacey."

And I wonder if I really am accomplishing anything or only frantically twirling a hamster wheel.

In the middle of all this, calmly ignoring the hustle of our lives, the blackberries steadily ripen. The closest ones grow along Powerline Road, beginning at the end of our little orchard and proceeding south, long determined vines twining high into the trees along the fencerow and snaking across the ditch and toward the road. Unlike the roses and corn, they ask nothing of us—no pruning, watering, or weeding. They simply produce countless rich purple berries, free for the taking.

I had sent the younger children out to pick a number of times this summer. They prefer the adventure of crossing the neighbor's field and picking in another patch along the railroad tracks, where they just might have the added excitement of seeing a fox or rabbit or even, one evening, the Barnum and Bailey circus train going by. They return with ice cream buckets full of blackberries that we turn into cobblers and pies or scoop into bags for the freezer.

But I had not yet gone picking myself, and a small prodding voice inside kept telling me I needed to, that this was important, that it wasn't about production and accomplishment, but that I needed the experience itself. So, finally, one evening after a day of canning green beans, I did. Nine-year-old Jenny was happy to go with me. We pulled on the boys' tall rubber boots and squelched out to the bushes just by the orchard.

Blackberry vines are nasty obstacles, studded with thorns that will snag a shirt or an arm and rip painfully. So picking requires patience and finesse, carefully threading a hand behind this vine, up over that one, and then yes!—there it is, the perfect berry dropped into the hand—and then slowly threading a cupped hand back out the way it came in. Despite my precautions, I kept snagging my hands and yelping.

"You don't have to say 'ouch' every time you get poked, you know," Jenny told me.

Of course she was right, this tomboy-princess daughter of mine, who seems to have far more stoic bravery than her mother ever did. Jenny and her blue bucket disappeared around the next bush. I kept picking, carefully, my amateur efforts nonetheless rewarded with a steady increase in the purple pile in my bucket.

A sense of restfulness and peace that I hadn't felt in weeks, maybe all summer, stole into my addled mind. I pulled leaves aside and admired the clusters of berries hiding behind them, beautiful and rich. I pushed vines aside with my rubber boots so I could reach deeper into the bush, and slowly I picked the berries that seemed to be waiting there, just for me, generous and free.

"I want to make my own pie this time," Jenny announced from farther down the ditch. My first response was a sigh— I really didn't have time to help her. But I knew I would anyhow; this was something I needed to do. We tallied our haul—plenty for a couple of pies at least—and went home, first picking a few more tantalizing berries that called to us and couldn't be ignored.

Back in the kitchen, I mixed the flour and shortening in a bowl and handed it to Jenny. She stirred in the cold water and squeezed the dough into a ball. Then she sprinkled flour on the table, rolled out a perfect piecrust, folded it in half, and settled it into the pie pan like she'd done this all her life.

Next she sliced off the edges with a butter knife and then pressed them into a pretty pattern with a fork. She measured and mixed the berry filling, poured it in, and cut decorative shapes from the leftover dough to place on top.

"Where in the world did you learn to do all that?" I asked, astonished.

"From watching you," she answered.

That was my blackberry moment, sweet and succulent. Good things are happening here, I realized, slowly ripening when I'm not looking, patiently developing among the grasping vines of busyness and demands, the thorns of mental lapses and my constant inability to catch up. Blackberries and children and the sweet things of life will not be rushed, and they will ripen in their own time, tasting of serenity and joy.

116

Slug Bugs and Family Traditions

"*B*eep Jeep!" my son Steven shouts from the back seat as he punches his brother, Ben, in the arm. "Ow!" Ben yells, then responds with a loud, "Hey! Slug bug!" and slugs Steven back.

The boys are 13 and 14, with long arms and legs sprawling all over the back seat. They see no need to corral their limbs, and 9-year-old Jenny, who is a third their size, often gets caught in the crossfire of their strange games.

Given the choice, this is not what I would have chosen as a family tradition. Perhaps a little song that we all sing in four-part harmony as we get into the car, that would be nice, or a ritual of identifying trees and cloud formations on the way to choir practice.

Instead, our family-in-the-car tradition is boys yelling and punching whenever they see a Jeep or Volkswagen Beetle. Often they add the disclaimer, "No take back!" to supposedly make them immune to revenge, but it doesn't work because the other brother mysteriously never hears it. Adding the color of a car adds an extra dimension to the experience, as in "Slug Bug yellow!" or "Beep Jeep blue!"

Then there's also the Smucker ritual of the digital Pioneer Villa sign, when we cross Interstate 5 on Highway 228, headed to Brownsville. Jenny gets involved just as enthusiastically as the boys, and they all elbow each other to get the best view, even going so far as to put their hands over their siblings' eyes to improve their own chances. Then they wait with bated breath through diesel prices and the little pitcher pouring coffee, so eagerly you'd think it was an oracle from the prophet Elijah himself that they were watching for, but actually, it's only the current temperature: "55 degrees! I saw it first!" "Nuh-uh! I did!" "No you did not!" "No fair, you pushed me!"

Back when I had just started out as a mom I would probably have tried to put a stop to these things before they ever became habitual—such violence and sheer foolishness. But now I tolerate the noisy games with patient amusement because I know I'm going to miss them when they're gone.

In the old days, really not that long ago, when the back seats were full of my older daughters and their friends in cotton school-uniform jumpers and long braids, the van would suddenly erupt in what sounded like noisy spitting whenever we passed a field with horses. "Slip slip slopsky!" "Slip slip slip!" A white horse was a "slopsky" and worth five points; anything else was "slip" and worth one. Whoever had the most points by the time we got to school won. A very odd game, I thought at the time, but now, whenever I pass the stables at the corner of Highway 228 and Falk Road, I brace just a bit for an eruption of slips and slopskys from the back seat that never comes. And I miss it.

The older I get, the more fond I am of tradition. Community traditions like the Fourth of July parade, church traditions like singing a capella hymns, family traditions in all their odd manifestations—these are good things. Traditions provide solid footing when life gets muddy and tell us who we are when we're no longer sure.

As a church, we Mennonites are good at tradition. The famous "Tradition!" song in *Fiddler on the Roof* was written of the Jewish community in Russia, but we're pretty sure we could offer them some stiff competition. Most of us chafe at this when we're about 17, including my daughter, Emily, who recently snorted that tradition is only a sign that people are afraid to change.

That was the age when I agitated about it as well, cramped by the rules of our Amish church. Plain, solid-color dresses, for instance, with no scope for personal expression. How stupid was that? There was nothing scriptural about it, I would fuss. "I mean, the Bible says, 'Consider the lilies, yet Solomon in all his glory was not arrayed like one of these,'" which was proof we should toss tradition aside and wear something pretty.

The world has spun around a few times and I have found that once you've survived financial difficulties and deathly ill children and deep disappointments, solid-color dresses are a non-issue and I could go back to them if that were the setting where I found purpose and belonging. After all, this is what tradition offers—something familiar and solid to fall back on, decided on by a group rather than one confused individual, a message that this is where I belong, this is what we do here, this is who we are.

I've found that church customs, while they serve a similar purpose as family traditions, evolve more slowly and are far more entrenched. Families are much more fluid, moving, in only 25 years or so, from a newly established home to having the oldest children grown up and gone.

Family traditions, I have found, often spring out of the moment, an impulsive decision that inadvertently becomes what we "always" do. And then, all too quickly, the children outgrow the custom and look back nostalgically, saying, "Remember how we always...?"

My husband, Paul, has read bedtime stories to the children ever since they were little. With three fiercely competitive children born in four years' time, the bedtime ritual turned into a complicated series of rules and turns: who got to sit on Dad's lap, who sat on either side, who could go hug Mom goodnight first, who got to stand on the orange chair to brush their teeth.

By now, of course, the need for such regulation is long gone. The three youngest still lounge on the couch to listen to a nightly story, the latest being *The Marvelous Inventions of Alvin Fernald*, and the older ones chuckle and recall, "Remember how Dad had to make all these rules so we wouldn't fight during the story, and the last one to hug Mom goodnight got to sit on Dad's lap the longest?"

In an effort to accustom our children to speaking in public, we used to take a bag of treats along to prayer meeting and afterward give them to any child who had quoted a Bible verse during "testimony" time. This led to one prayer-meeting leader rapturously praising our children, who had just burst out popcorn-like with Bible verses. I thought, but did not say, "Brother, don't be too impressed; we have chocolate waiting in the van."

When our finances improved, this custom slowly changed into ice cream bars at the Shell station on the way home for anyone who either said a verse or led in prayer. Changing it now would be unthinkable. It's a family tradition, it's what we do, and the clerks at the Shell station have been known to watch for us on Wednesday nights. And it has served its purpose: Our children aren't afraid to speak up in public. This is part of who they are, thanks to a seemingly insignificant family tradition.

I have a hard time imagining anything profoundly redemptive ever coming out of my children watching for the temperature on the Pioneer Villa sign or hollering when they see a Jeep. But I am certain that when they're all grown up they will cross the overpass at Interstate 5 and remember, laughing, how they were long-legged kids in the back seat, punching each other. We were a family, and this is who we were, and this is what we did, and it all had a part in who they eventually became.

Making Peace With Change

I wish a bell would ring to warn me whenever my life is about to change. Not only before big calamities, but also when I've settled into a nice routine and am about to be jolted out of it.

There was no indication that anything would be different that morning last week when I put the three youngest children and a pile of buckets in the van and we headed out to a strawberry patch, just as we have done every June for the last 14 years. I wore my old denim skirt and stained shirt that I always wear, happy in the knowledge that I've finally learned how to do this well—when to go, how many to pick, how to motivate the children.

We drove the country roads to a farm near the west end of Cartney Drive. There, the children reluctantly emerged from the van, nearly locking the keys inside, as always, and we weighed our buckets under a canopy cluttered with berry-stained buckets and boxes. Shivering in the chilly morning air, we followed the rows down to the little orange flags, pushed the dewy leaves aside, admired the wealth of shiny red berries, and began to pick. Then, knowing how quickly children tire of berry-picking, I reminded them, in my oh-won't-this-be-fun voice, of the incentive that I have used successfully for years. "Remember, every time you pick 50 berries, you get to throw one at me."

"Yeah, Mom, we know."

After a quarter-bucket, I looked around. No berries had yet come flying my way. Hmmm, strange.

Five minutes later Jenny, age 9, gleefully threw a squashed berry in my direction and groaned when it missed me by five feet. Steven and Ben, aged 13 and 14, quietly kept picking. A few minutes later a berry hit my back and Jenny shrieked with joy, but the boys showed no reaction.

Impossibly soon, the boys and I had each filled a bucket. We helped Jenny finish hers and then quickly filled a fifth bucket and carried them to the canopy to weigh and pay. Chitchat with the farmer, pull out the cash with red-stained fingers—all was as it ought to be. We started for home. "So," I said to the boys, "I noticed you didn't throw any berries at me."

They shrugged.

"So what's with that?" I pressed.

"I dunno." They stared out the window, bored. "Do you know what time Dad wants us at the warehouse today?"

I drove on past fields heavy with the reliable green gold of late June, feeling like an era was coming to an end and a clever-mom idea, of which I had had so few, had turned into something silly, useful only with Jenny now, but probably not for long. Why, I wondered, do things have to keep changing on me just as I finally get them figured out?

Our family e-mail account, for instance. There was no warning about this, either, or else I would have made a backup as everyone ought to but most of us find out the hard way. Ten years ago my husband was all excited about the amazing possibilities of hooking our computer to the phone, which would open up something called the Internet. It all sounded vaguely dangerous to me, so he said he would wait until I felt comfortable with it. Finally, my gift to him one

Christmas, probably one of his favorite ever, was permission to buy a modem. My motive was partially selfish, as I vaguely understood that this might make it easier to communicate with my sister in Yemen.

First we had a primitive fax program, and not long after, we advanced to Juno, an efficient and easy-to-use program that let me send and receive e-mails. It wasn't difficult to master, and at last I could communicate quickly and inexpensively with my sister. The days of two-week delays with letters and $1.50-a-minute phone calls were over. At first it seemed everyone had Juno, but then others in my life advanced to fancier programs. Later, for my teenagers, e-mail became passé and they communicated via Xanga messages and texting on their cell phones.

But I stuck with my old, basic version of Juno. I liked it, it worked, it didn't come up with new options, and I had all the messages stored on our computer instead of, as I imagined, some damp warehouse in Seattle, all of which came back to bite me when it suddenly overloaded its capacity and locked up tight.

Our son, Matt, calmly rescued what he could, which wasn't much, and I knew the time had come for something different.

"Gmail, definitely Gmail," said helpful young friends. "Yahoo, with Outlook or Thunderbird" said others.

Reluctantly, I checked them out. It was overwhelming. Click here for weather in Harrisburg, there for world news, over here for entertainment. Faces popped up on the sidebar to tell me what to take for asthma or heartburn. Did I want to chat? asked this button. Or invite a friend? offered that one.

Like a frightened kindergartener on her first day of school, I didn't want any of it. "Just take me home," I wanted to wail, "back to how it's always been."

Maybe my resistance to change is cultural, like the joke my brother likes to tell: "How many Mennonites does it take to change a light bulb?" Answer: "Change?"

Or perhaps it's a normal feature of the post-40 landscape.

For whatever reason, I find myself fighting change, unable to reconcile myself to it, and having to be yanked or shoved into the future. Sometimes, however, I am reminded that what is familiar to me now was once unfamiliar, and that my life is what it is today because of a long series of mostly unwelcome changes. I was invited last winter to speak to a group of third-graders in Santa Clara about being an author. I told them about my Amish background, and how, when I was their age, I learned to write letters to Grandma because you can't pick up the phone and call Grandma when you're Amish.

I also told them about my current writing projects, including the fact that I have a blog that they can look up on the Internet and read a new entry every few days. I started this at the insistence of a nephew who had one before anyone else did, it seemed, and who kept saying, "Aunt Dorcas, you need a blog," and showed me how to get started.

Afterward, one of the teachers remarked, "Isn't it amazing—how far you've come, and how your life has changed?"

"Changed?"

"Yes. Think about it. You went from being this Amish girl who didn't know how to use a phone, to having a computer and a—what's it called? A blog?—I hardly even know what that is."

Of course she was right. Many of the things I enjoy today—laughing with my young-adult children, talking on my cell phone, new messages in my inbox—came about because of change, most of which I resisted.

If nothing ever changed, my old e-mail program would still work when I'm 70, and my sons would be middle-aged men, meekly following me to the berry patch and tossing a strawberry my way every time they picked 50.

I know that life will keep changing and no bells will ring to warn me ahead of time. My family will keep dragging me into the future. And long after the fact I will finally make peace with change and recognize that perhaps it was really for the best after all.

Passing On the Story Heirlooms

A few days after Christmas, I gave my daughter a precious family heirloom disguised as a simple story.

Seven-year-old Jenny was sick with the flu but improving just enough to be grumpy and bored. "Adventures in Odyssey," hot chocolate, and Ramona Quimby had exhausted their appeal, and only one thing would do: a story from Mom. So I left the dishes, snuggled on the couch with her, and told her the story of my grandma and the windmill. Grandma always told us the story in Pennsylvania German, so I used some of the same phrases.

Grandma was probably 5 years old, I told Jenny, and her family lived out in the country but I'm not sure where, since they moved around so much. She had an older brother, Noah, who was like many big brothers, and he told Grandma that if she climbed up to the top of the windmill, or the *vint-boomp*, she would see a wolf! Except that Grandma always stretched out the German word — *voolllllllffff*.

Grandma knew better, of course, but she really wanted to see a wolf, so up she went. There was no wolf to be seen anywhere, but suddenly the wind whipped her dress forward and it caught on the center of the turning blades. The windmill turned around and around, and Grandma couldn't get away. It twisted her skirt, tighter and tighter, and she was scared half to death, or as she put it, *halp-doat faschruka*. Finally, the fabric gave way and a large piece ripped out of her dress. Grandma climbed down the windmill, shaking, and there her mother spanked her half to death, *halp-doat*, she claimed. And then they somehow retrieved the torn piece of fabric and her mother mended the dress so Grandma could wear it again.

And then, of course, I had to tell Jenny the rest of the story—how my sister and I reacted to Grandma's story when we were little girls.

"But Grandma," we always protested at this point. "That couldn't be! If you were scared half to death, and then your mother spanked you half to death, you'd be all dead!"

But Grandma never wavered in her story. No, she insisted, that's how it was—first she was *halp-doat faschrucka*, and then her mother spanked her *halp-doat*.

I finished the story and Jenny grinned despite her sore throat and miserable cough. "A *vint-boomp*?" she croaked, trying out the new word. "And a *volf*?" She giggled, working her mind around the idea of her mom and Aunt Becky trying to get their old Amish grandma to see the logic of half-dead plus half-dead equalling all-dead.

Emily, who is 16, was also listening. "I think that would be cool to tell your grandchildren stories that your grandma told you," she said.

"I think so, too," I said, realizing that I was actually looking forward to this.

The truth has been slowly dawning, lately, that I may soon be entering a new phase of my life. I do not enjoy change and am usually the last one to acknowledge that the wind is shifting. My youngest child is barely in school, I feel like I have only just now figured out how to be a mom, but I can no longer ignore the signs that new experiences are inevitably ahead.

For one thing, a sudden swarm of my children's friends are dating, and three different cousins announced their engagements in the past few weeks. Courtship, among conservative Mennonites, is generally not undertaken for its own sake but as the means to an end. So teens tend to begin dating at an older age than the average (at least 18) and marry younger, often in their early 20s, a system that seems to result in a remarkably large percentage of long-term, successful marriages. This means that, since my older children are 20 and 18, the topic is on their minds. But it was something I conveniently told myself was still far off in a hazy future for us, Matt and Amy thankfully being busy with other pursuits.

But at our Christmas dinner I was drawn up short with just how close this possibility might be. After the pumpkin pie, we talked about what our family would be like 10 years from now and wrote down our predictions, to be read at our Christmas dinner in 2016. "This table will need to be bigger," Matt said. Amy added, "There will definitely be a few kids running around." Paul guessed that he and I would have three in-laws and three grandchildren.

None of the others seemed to think this remarkable, but I, as usual, was the one "freaking out," as my children say. "I could be a mother-in-law and a grandma in the next 10 years? Ten years is nothing!" I bleated. "But ... but I don't know how to be a grandma!"

"Oh, Mom, you'll be a good grandma," Amy assured me. "You'll tell lots of stories."

How sweet of my daughter to zero in on the one thing that I have in abundance and do as naturally as breathing, and to reassure me of its value. Heaven knows, I probably will never pass along land, like my husband's grandpa did, or quilts and rag rugs like my mom, or money or silver tea sets or recipes or prize-winning roses. But I have hundreds of stories filed away, and in this area, more than any other, I trust my skills and ability.

Telling Jenny about my grandma and the windmill is much more than a moment's distraction from the flu. It is telling her, subtly, that she is connected to people of long ago who were once children just like her, that behavior has consequences, that even a sad story can become funny in its own way many years later. A story is much more than just a story; it is a connection, a reassurance, a lesson, a door opening. It can last for years and stay fresh and fascinating. It is a mystery—why do I gravitate to tell this story and not that one?

Through stories, I hope to pass on what's most important—faith in God, love, hope for the future. When I tell of how our lives were spared when we hit a moose and our van burned up, I am saying, without actually saying, "God is real. He still does miracles."

One of the most remarkable characteristics of a story is how it gathers layers, snowball-like, as it rolls along. My older children loved the story of when I was a child and Alexander, our cat, died, and my sisters and I had a funeral, with Becky wearing a filmy black scarf over her face like Jackie Kennedy and Margaret carrying the sad little box. I had made up a song for the occasion, to the tune of "Father I Stretch My Hands to Thee": "To you dear Alexander cat, we sing our lonely song. But we are also thankful that we had you for this long," and so on.

But my younger children equally love the next layer of the story: how their tough older brother, Matt, when he was about 6 years old, would beg me to tell this story even though he always broke down and cried when I sang the funeral dirge. "Why did he keep wanting to hear it?" they say, and I don't know. And they smile, the sadness of it all somehow turning into something special.

And Grandma's story of the windmill now includes my reaction to it as a child, trying to teach Grandma math and logic. I hope that someday, years from now, Jenny adds another layer to it, snuggling with her grandchildren. "Many years ago when I was sick with the flu, my mom sat with me on a blue plaid couch, and she told me a story about her grandma and a *vint-boomp.*"

To Each, Her Own Snow Memories

For some reason my children have never been as impressed as I think they ought to be that I survived Minnesota's "Blizzard of the Century" in January 1975. At least once per winter, when we get just enough snow to cover the sidewalk, I lapse into rambling memories of that adventure.

"Mom and Becky and Margaret and I were home alone for most of it," I say, "in that old house we were renting, you know, down the road from where Grandpa and Grandma live now. Dad and Marcus stayed over at the new house to take care of the animals. Nobody knew it was coming, and they sent us home from school an hour after we got there, and it was snowing like crazy already.

"The wind blew so hard that this gritty snow blew in around the storm windows and the plastic over the outside and everything, and when we got up in the morning there were little piles of snow on the windowsills. We all slept downstairs to stay warm. Margaret remembers that the cylinders in the oil stove glowed red-hot and Mom was worried about the house burning down.

"When the storm was finally over there were drifts outside 10 and 15 feet high, and we could walk right on top of them without sinking down. It was like this bizarre world out there. We walked up on a drift higher than the top of the chicken house, and out by the field you could see a row of fence posts sticking up three inches out of the snow."

At this point I am lost in vivid memories—seeing that strange landscape, feeling the cold wind—but their eyes are glazing over. "Yes, Mom, and you and Aunt Becky got so bored in the middle of the storm you decided to bake something," they say, no doubt thinking to themselves, "and then, Grandma, you walked 5 miles to school, uphill both ways."

No matter how often I try or how many adjectives I use, I seem unable to convey to my Oregon-grown children the intensity of that storm, the dangers, the isolation, the cold, the family bonding around the stove, and the sense, afterwards, that we had survived something terrible together. Online resources confirm my memories, thankfully, so I know it wasn't just an exaggerated perception in my 12-year-old mind. The wind gusts reached 70 to 90 miles per hour and produced snowdrifts up to 20 feet high, Wikipedia tells me. "The combination of snowfall totals, wind velocities, and cold temperatures made this one of the worst blizzards the upper Midwest has experienced."

Why is it that, much as they enjoy stories from when I was young, the children yawn through this one? Maybe snow is something that you can't explain: You simply have to experience it for yourself.

When an unusual snowstorm hit the Willamette Valley recently, it wasn't anything like that famous blizzard. However, as I compared the two, I discovered a few similarities, and came to the surprising conclusion that my children found the recent storm as impressive and full of adventure—and would probably remember it as vividly—as I do that long-ago event.

This storm, for example, was just as unexpected as that one, with no indication that Saturday night's rain would turn to snow. We woke up expecting our normal Sunday-morning bustle to get ready for church, and were surprised to see a thick, steady snow falling, with everything but a few green circles under the pine trees already turned white.

How quickly a normal morning can be turned upside-down, the rain turned to snow, the green to white, and—impossible thought—would we stay home from church? Sunday morning services for our family are as dependable as the tides. They always are. And, barring sickness, we always attend.

The boys dressed in khaki pants and buttoned shirts. My husband, Paul, and I watched the snow accumulate. Finally, after a flurry of phone calls, the decision was made: Church was canceled, the only time in my kids' memory that this had ever happened. Gleefully, they hauled winter supplies from the attic, traded dress clothes for snowsuits, and stomped outside to pound each other with snowballs and build large snowmen with stick arms and billed Trailblazer caps.

Canceling services because of the weather wasn't that unusual in Minnesota, but I remember that the difference during that blizzard was this: It was the only time in my life that church was canceled and no one phoned to say so. Everyone just knew.

A strange sort of boredom sets in when the weather confines you at home. Blizzard syndrome, I call it, remembering how antsy we got by the second day. Becky remembers that Mom tried to come up with activities, and we sat around the stove and played who-what-where, each of us writing down a noun, passing the paper on, and adding verbs and adverbs, and then laughing crazily at the resulting sentences.

The baking project, as I recall, was our idea. Becky and I flipped through Mom's collection of magazine recipes and chose Prune Loaf, which probably tells a lot about our food supply, but which turned out surprisingly good: the stewed prunes wrapped in sugary pieces of dough and baked in a loaf pan.

My husband staved off blizzard syndrome at our house by playing games with the kids whenever they came inside to warm up. They played a Monopoly game from start to finish, and I joined them for a three-hour Phase-10 marathon, whirring fruit smoothies in the blender for everyone between turns. "Just think of all the memories we're making!" 17-year-old Emily gushed. "Dad's home all day. How often does that happen? And making smoothies, and playing games, and those huge snowmen. And all our good arguments—we'll always remember this!"

Who but a Smucker would consider our silly arguments good memories? Emily insisted, for instance, that rain was better than snow, and more romantic besides. "Wouldn't it be romantic to be proposed to in the rain?"

"With water dripping off your nose?" I snapped. "No. Romantic would be to be proposed to in the twilight, in the gently falling snow."

"Oh, Mom!"

A large machine rumbled by outside. "Hey, the snowplow just went!" Ben said.

"Snowplow?" Paul said. "That was the road grader. Snowplows are trucks with blades on the front and a load of sand in the back."

"What?" I said. "Snowplows are big yellow machines. How on Earth would a truck have made it through those big drifts after our blizzard? Even the snowplow had to back off and then rev up to get through those drifts, and the snow at the side was piled as high as the top of the school bus when we finally went back to school," I went on, as usual adding more details than anyone wanted to hear.

Our children missed only one day of school and then went back on Tuesday, after most of the snow had melted off the roads.

What will Oregon be like by the time my children have children? I wonder. I imagine Emily, at a sunny mid-February picnic, reminiscing: "Did I ever tell you about the big snow of 2008? We all stayed home from church, and Ben and Steven made these big snowmen, and..."

"Yes, Mom, we know," her kids will say, rolling their eyes. "You all played Phase 10 at the kitchen table and argued about snowplows."

Or maybe, in the middle of the Willamette Valley's Blizzard of the 21st Century, Ben's children will say: "Remember how Dad always thought it was so cool that he survived that 5-inch snow back in 2008?"

And gathered around the stove, they will all laugh, warm and safe inside as the cold wind howls and the drifts pile thickly against the house.

Going On and
Giving Back

Tailored Sensibilities

I have a house to decorate, and I am drowning in adjectives and advice.

At Jerry's Home Improvement Center, below hundreds of little square paint samples, I found a quiz to help me discover my "color personality." Since I would like my living room to feel "relaxed and inviting," I am told that my personality is "casual," which can be subdivided into "romantic," "charming," and "cozy," with a separate booklet of paint swatches for each.

I also have a touch of "timeless," the quiz tells me. "Shadowy green and burnished gold fit your tailored sensibilities."

For 95 years, our kitchen and living room were two separate rooms connected by a narrow doorway. They were designed by my husband Paul's great-grandfather, who had simple, straightforward tastes rather than tailored sensibilities. I can imagine him quickly sketching a square in a notebook, drawing a line down the middle from top to bottom, crossing it with another going left and right, repeating it for the upstairs, and there he was. A good Mennonite house for a family of 12. No need to be fancy. His wife, I am guessing, persuaded him to add the few extra touches: a bay window and bead-board wainscoting. The bay window remains intact but the wainscoting was covered with Sheetrock some 20 years ago by my husband's dad, who was as practical and un-fancy as his grandfather.

Despite the boxy rooms and annoying layout, I am fond of this house, preferring history and personality to convenience and artistic design. Soon after we moved in six years ago, we hung garage-sale wallpaper in the living room and put down a linoleum remnant in the kitchen. Our furniture tastes featured a comfortable selection of classified-ad finds and Early Salvation Army.

A few weeks ago, Paul took out half of the wall between the kitchen and living room, and suddenly the downstairs seemed twice as spacious and bright. Then he tore up the carpet, put down laminate wood-look flooring in both rooms, and restored the bead-board wainscoting. The result was a large cohesive room that begged for a whole new look. It was time for serious redecorating.

I had saved up for this, and I knew what I wanted: Something authentic yet up-to-date; something harmonious and simple; not makeshift, not elaborate, but with understated good taste.

Unfortunately, I had no idea how to get from here to there.

Among my daughters and friends I am known for being hopelessly behind the times, wearing my skirts firmly cinched at the waist, rather than two inches below, and using orange and avocado green Tupperware long after the rest of the world has moved to blush, seafoam, or crimson. To leap from years of out-of-fashion decorating to the surreal world of Ralph Lauren paint and Broyhill furniture is to encounter an unimaginable number of choices that collectively freeze, rather than free, the imagination.

At Home Depot, I wandered through sample kitchens and was handed catalogs with stunning combinations of Corian countertops, slide-out spice shelves, and hardwood wine racks. Instead of envy or desire, all I could think of was, "No one ever filled bummer-lamb bottles in that kitchen."

Later, I stepped into the posh atmosphere of a furniture store the size of a Boeing hangar and as dim and hushed as a funeral parlor. There I found a couch and loveseat I liked— for $2,200. With three boys who drape and flop and perch but seldom actually sit, I would be insane to come home with $2,200 furniture.

"I think if you find stuff you think is pretty and put it together, it'll look nice," said my 15-year-old daughter, Emily. "Not everything has to match and stuff, you know."

"Easy for you to say," I sniffed, and went to a secondhand store and bought a stack of magazines with such names as *Cottage Living* and *Farmhouse Decorating* to guide me in my quest of getting it right.

That's when the trickle of adjectives and advice became a river.

"Earthy colors look dark and cavelike," one designer said. Another insisted I need a "lush floral motif" with "maximized romance." But not a "saccharine" or "fussy" living room, I was warned. I could achieve a "zesty atmosphere" with "turquoise cushions" and "airy window treatments."

Two pages later, the floral motif was out and character was in. I must have "soothing" blue and green stripes, "prim panels" and "cultured curtains."

By this time, a little warning light was flashing in my head. Something about all this seemed wrong, but I wasn't sure what it was. Then, a "before" picture showed a bedroom that, among many other faults, had a "nasty mauve carpet." "Hey!" I said, not quite out loud. "I like mauve!" It wasn't that long ago when *Cottage Living* featured mauve and country blue as authentic and charming, indispensible to the country/farmhouse look. And now mauve was suddenly nasty? Who changed the rules while I wasn't looking?

Somebody, I suspected, was having too much fun at my expense. Perhaps there was no science or right and wrong to this, after all, only people stating their opinions as though they were law and trying to get me to spend a lot of money redecorating every few years.

I began to read the magazines with a skeptical eye. A set of dreadful vases was described as gorgeous and elegant. I visualized three young magazine people around a table, working on an assignment. "OK," one says, "let's get a bunch of these ugly vases from my grandma, ceramic with gold trim and big pink flowers stuck on the side."

"Yeah," says another, "and let's arrange them on these shelves where, if this were a real house, everyone coming through the door would knock them down. Then let's call them, oh, how about 'cute'?" (She flips through her thesaurus.) "No no, 'gorgeous.'"

"And elegant," says the third. "We haven't used 'elegant' on this page yet."

"Oh yeah, and I found this creepy green paint for the walls. We'll call it restful and classic."

"Really, Mom," Emily insisted, "if you put stuff together that's pretty to you, it'll look nice. You don't have to worry about what anyone else thinks. Have you seen my bookshelves?"

I had. They contained her collection of old hardcover fairy tales accented with a pink straw hat, a black elephant carving from Kenya, a modern-art sculpture from my welder brother, and a purple-and-black set of nesting "Russian" dolls from Poland. The whole effect was, as the magazines would say, quirky, original, and harmonious.

Now that I have been a mom for 20 years, the advice I most often give to younger mothers is to trust their instincts, the heart-sense that tells them what's right. Strangely, in this area, it was my daughter teaching me the same thing. Perhaps, like her, I should start with what I already had and loved, such as the seascape in oils that I picked up for $5. I could pull a shade of blue from it to paint the wainscoting and a second shade for the trim.

How liberating to assign my own adjectives and write my own advice. If the right color turns out to be an out-of-style "country" blue, so what? I have tailored sensibilities, after all, and if I decide to call it soothing and cultured, that's precisely what it will be.

Once Upon a
Writing Class

The books say I should start with a main character who has a problem to solve.

All right, then, I am the main character: Mrs. Smucker, a much-too-busy, forgetful, 40-something mom. And I have a problem to solve: I am supposed to teach eight teenagers how to write fiction, and I don't know anything about writing fiction.

My husband, Paul, as principal, made a new drive this year to get the students' parents to volunteer at our church school. So Rachel and Rita teach an art class, Bonnie and Sharon listen to children read, and Regina helps with cleaning.

And I am supposed to teach the older students how to write.

We have four weeks of classes in the fall and begin with blog posts, an easy choice: I know how to write them, and blogs are relevant to teenagers. "yo my sweet peeps im gonna hang out at jessica's" is not communication, I tell them. "Write a post that actually says something." They dutifully crank out thoughtful essays that will most likely never be equalled on any actual blogs in the teenage universe.

After a two-month recess, it is time to write fiction. I would rather eat a piece of cheesecake, creamy and rich, with a hint of sour cream and raspberries, than figure out how to make it myself. How many eggs? How do I keep the crumbs from getting soggy? Similarly, I would rather curl up in a chair and read a good story than figure out how the author made it work. The *No. 1 Ladies Detective Agency* series, for example, a recently discovered literary treasure. How does the author create suspense? What words make the personality of Precious Ramotswe come alive? Why is this episode inserted here and not three chapters later? What makes me keep reading?

I gather books with hopeful and ambitious titles: *Any Child Can Write; What's Your Story?* and *Writing Smarts—A Girl's Guide to Writing Great Poetry, Stories, School Reports, and More!*

A story begins with a character; the books all agree on this. He or she has specific characteristics such as red hair, stubbornness, and a fear of heights. The character wants something badly or has a problem to solve. He can't solve his problems too easily, or it's not a good story.

I may be the main character in my story, but there are eight secondary characters with a wide range of skills and passions. Two of my children represent opposite ends of the writing spectrum. Emily, who is 16, has so many ideas flying by that all she has to do is reach out and grab the nearest one. She journals prolifically and owns 70 notebooks. Her prize possession is an old green Royal typewriter from her grandparents. At the other end is Ben, age 13, who fills his head with basketball and math. He multiplies multi-digit numbers in his head, but the smallest writing assignment in history or English makes him flop backward on the couch and writhe and grimace as though dying of appendicitis.

"But it doesn't make any sense!" he wails. "I don't know what to write."

In addition to characters, the books say, every story needs a setting. Ours is a bit dull but functional – on chairs around the Sunday school table in the church fellowship hall, two afternoons a week, the thermostat turned down too low, little first-graders peeking in the windows during their break.

I am determined to make the class enjoyable for everyone, writers and nonwriters alike. But, lest this story resolve itself too easily, the first session sets an unexpected bump in my path: Justin and Preston simply won't be quiet. Their murmured asides and choked giggles continue despite my hints and glares. I ding the little teacher's bell in front of me, even though each ding reduces their three allotted good-behavior Hershey Kisses by one.

Later, at home, Paul offers to step in and rescue me, but main characters need to solve their own problems, the books say.

At the next class, I seat Justin on my right and Preston to my left. I also hand out copies of The Rules: "When Mrs. Smucker is talking, no one else talks. When something is funny, we share it with the whole class." It works. From then on, all is well and everyone takes his turn to talk.

We begin by creating characters. Kayla forms "Alaiya," who is 22 years old, wears sweatshirts, and dislikes loud kids. Alaiya wants her students to learn, but they won't listen to her.

Hmmm, I think. I wonder where Kayla got this idea.

The boys' characters are all sports-related. Justin concocts "Travis" who wants to play basketball at UCLA but isn't good enough. The kids' characters are OK but bland, lacking what the books call "juicy details" and "a little zip."

So we head down a side road to learn description. I hand out a list of words and we expand them into sentences that "pop."

Drennan turns "dog" and "cat" into "The huge, fierce-looking, short-haired dog growled at the ugly, flea-bitten stray cat."

We are going places, I'm sure of it.

Finally, it's time to write some actual stories. On a computer, if possible, I say. And about 400 words. I suggest an optional opening line: "Mrs. Finkelstein's dentures were missing."

"Do we have to count every single word?" they wonder.

"Does this have to be something that could really happen?"

"What shall I do cuz I'm staying at my grandma's house and she doesn't have a computer?"

"Just write a story," I say.

And they do.

When I get up at 6:30 one morning, Ben is at the computer, happily typing without a single moan or complaint. As I read over his shoulder, he chuckles and adds another twist in the plot—Mrs. Finkelstein finally finds her dentures on the nightstand, but in her excitement she falls out of bed and breaks her hip.

We read and review the stories in class, and I am thrilled. Stephanie's is full of realistic dialogue and a perfect ending. Preston's story is about football and full of action. "'Let's run a counter right,' Cam said. The play was not a success, and they got stuffed at the line of scrimmage."

Emily begins, "Mrs. Finkelstein's dentures were missing. All 72 pairs were gone."

I take the papers home and grade them, muttering "Yes!"
"Wow, look at this." "Amazing."

Then I tuck the papers in a folder and smile.

The end.

Stepping Between Two Worlds

I operate in two completely different worlds, living in one and visiting the other.

The first is my world as a wife and mom in the middle of summer's grass fields and busyness. I never know what waits for me when I get up in the morning. It might be our enormous dog, Hansie, lying on his bed and chewing on pink and blue birthday candles. With detective skills from 22 years of mothering, I deduce that this was the combined work of my two teenage boys and, of course, the dog, each of whom weigh about 150 pounds and have big feet, bigger appetites, and a streak of mischief.

Ben, I recall, had accidentally dumped the bin of party supplies in the back pantry the day before and then assured me he picked them all up. Then Steven took the pop cans out the back door to the car, and didn't latch the door behind him, an error that Hansie always catches, and which has previously resulted in the disappearance of a large container of homemade chocolate chip cookies and an 8-pound beef roast.

So, I gather, Ben didn't pick up the bags of candles and little pastel candleholders, Steven left the door unlatched, and Hansie found something new and incongruous to chew on. A typical beginning to a typical day in my everyday universe.

This world is full of people this summer—my husband and me, six children, and a seed-sacking teenage nephew named Zack. I feel like I live at the Portland airport: Flight 63 exiting by the back door with a jug of ice water, Flight 144 coming in hot and dusty at the front, Flight 26 strapping on his bike helmet and preparing for takeoff.

Harvest brings an increase in activity, dirt, and appetites. Steven grills 20 hamburgers for lunch and they all disappear by 3 p.m. Ryegrass seeds spill out of pockets and lie scattered on the bathroom floor after showers, to sprout from under the baseboards next winter.

I don't always feel appreciated here. My daughters giggle at my memory lapses and say, "Wow, Mom, you're getting a lot of gray hair!" The boys seem to perceive me as an invisible motor that keeps things fed and cleaned but doesn't require much attention. I try to say profound motherly things at the supper table and no one hears me.

Then suddenly, in the middle of laundry or dishes or weeding flower beds, I know it's time. I kick off the muddy garden shoes and head for the shower. Then I slip into shoes with heels that click and a coordinated outfit with no spaghetti-sauce stains on the front or flower-bed dirt on the knees. A quick fluff in my hair and a spritz of hairspray, hollered last-minute instructions to bake the lasagna for an hour and gather the eggs, and I roll my tote of books through the kitchen and am off to visit my other universe.

My Kia Optima is a golden chariot, transporting me to distant galaxies, transforming me from hassled mom to cool, Professional Author. I set the seat and the temperature exactly where I like them, turn off the K-Love station, pop in a CD of melodious a capella gospel songs by the Nathan Good Family, and head down Powerline Road and into the sunshine, singing along if the mood strikes me.

These venues vary from library fundraisers to Lions Club meetings to Bible studies at YaPoAh Terrace. Invariably, an eager woman is waiting at the door. "Oh, I'm so glad to meet you!" she says. "Can I help you with your bag? Here, let me take that." Other equally eager people greet me inside. They are glad to see me, they have read my writings, they bought my book to send to a daughter in Michigan. I am settled into the best chair in the house. Would I like coffee? Or perhaps a cup of tea? Cream or sugar? Would I like a special sort of pen for signing books?

I sip my drink and look around. Everyone in the room is polite and quiet and civilized, the outfits are clean and well-coordinated, there isn't a speck of warehouse dust in sight. People chat about things that belong in this universe — a new tea shop downtown, the latest politics, the symphony on Tuesday night.

"I bought a pint of organic blueberries," I hear a woman say, and I wonder what it would be like to get a pint of fruit instead of multiple gallons.

Soon it's time for my talk, and for the first time in weeks I actually have the attention of everyone in the room. I get to say exactly what I want, and except for the inevitable white-haired gentleman who falls asleep, everyone listens with such full attention that I begin to think I might actually be saying something worthwhile. No one interrupts, no one hollers across the table, no one argues with my conclusions. And at the end they all applaud. People begin to mill around as I sit down to sign books. One by one, they stop by to thank me or buy books or tell me that they had an Amish great-uncle-by-marriage in Ohio by the name of Smucker or Schmucker and, oh what was it, John, or Jake? At least two women tell me I look far too young to have six children. I start conversations and finish them. Everyone is nice.

And then, like the final bite of pumpkin pie with whipped cream at Thanksgiving dinner, I am suddenly utterly satisfied and I know one more sugary bite would mean illness. Everything has been compliments, delight, and affirmation. And it's enough. Time to go.

I tuck my things in the backpack and roll it out to the Kia. Too tired mentally even for music, I drive home in silence, pondering, leaving that universe behind, rolling through a galaxy or two to return to the other. The boys are shooting baskets when I drive in, and a stray shot bounces off the car with a clang. Hansie nudges my hand and drools happily on my lovely skirt as I get out of the car. I click through the kitchen, noting empty ice cube trays scattered on the island, newspapers on the table, enormous sandals tossed by the front door.

"Mom! You're supposed to call Grandma!" a voice shouts from upstairs. "Mom, I'm hungry!" "Hey, has anyone seen today's mail?" "Mom, did you mend my warehouse pants?" "Mom, can I buy a .22?" "Oh, Mom, I forgot to tell you—Coffeys need someone to feed the chickens tomorrow."

A homemade arrow flies past me and hits my desk. I turn to see Jenny showing off her new bow made of a stick and string. The back door slams, the phone rings, and there's a terrible crash upstairs.

I change into comfortable denim, steer one boy toward the empty ice cube trays and the other toward the pile of shoes by the door, send Jenny and her arrows outside, tell Amy to pack a lunch for Zack the nephew, call upstairs to ask Emily if she gathered the laundry, kiss the dusty husband coming in the door, and grab the phone to call Grandma.

The gentle sweetness of my other universe seems far away. I roll up my sleeves and smile. I'm ready for this again, back in my everyday world, back where life is wild and noisy and challenging, back where I'm needed, back with the ones I love, back where I love to be.

What Love
Looks Like

*M*y husband, Paul, and I sit in our office chairs, temporarily distracted from his bookkeeping and my computer, and talk about all the things a minister/grass-seed-guy and his wife need to discuss—church schedules, teenagers, employees. Pigga the cat wanders in and hops on Paul's lap. Seemingly unaware of her, he keeps talking, but slowly begins to smooth her fluffy gray fur and gently stroke her back.

Watching, I think: This is what love looks like; this is what it does.

With Valentine's Day coming soon, every store from WinCo to Goodwill to—who knows, maybe even Les Schwab Tire Center—has a prominent aisle exploding in a red-and-white celebration of romance. In contrast, the latest *National Geographic* magazine features a scientific study of love, reducing it to biochemistry—serotonin levels and the "surge and pulse of dopamine." Falling out of love is as inevitable as falling in, we are told, coldly.

Love is an elusive thing, defying description—part emotion, part decision, part something that can't be reduced to candy hearts or chemicals. I prefer to define it, as the Bible does, in action terms: it suffers long, it is kind, it does not seek its own way.

For me, love is best illustrated by the story of two cats and my husband.

Paul has never been an animal guy, one to talk to dogs and scratch cats between the ears. He wasn't the sort of man who kicked cats, or I would never have married him; he was simply indifferent to them. When a black-and-white cat showed up at our doorstep five years ago, Paul said he didn't mind if she stayed, as long as we kept her outside where he could ignore her at will. We named her Katzie, and for years she was queen—lying on the porch in the sun, getting fat, and catching mice only when she felt like it.

Then an enormous German shepherd-mix named Hansie joined our family last November, and Katzie's life changed completely. Instead of living in peace and plumpness, she was on the run, flying headlong around the corner of the house and scampering up a tree with Hansie behind her taking the corner on two wheels and woofing ferociously.

Any cat, it seems, could have known that this place was no longer hospitable. But on a cold, rainy day early in December, the children found a tiny, wet, stray kitten wedged under the heating-oil tank beside the house. Fifteen-year-old Emily knelt in the mud, worked her arm under the tank, and pulled it out. She shampooed and blow-dried the pathetic, oily kitten in the bathroom sink, transforming it into a round gray fluff with stubby legs.

Emily named it Pigga, not because it was shaped like a piggy bank but because it was found under the oil tank. "See, I always thought that tank looked like a big pig, and when I was little I used to say 'pigga' instead of 'pig.'"

Pigga needed to stay indoors a few days to recover, and Paul, who is tough at times but not heartless, saw the sense in this. But we soon realized sending Pigga outside would turn her into instant catburger. Whenever Hansie looked in the patio doors and saw the kitten run across the floor, he crashed into the glass and burst into a frenzy of angry barking.

"German shepherds are death on cats," warned my friend, Rachel. "Ours killed the cat two minutes after we let her outside."

So Pigga stayed inside, leaping at skirt hems and dangling backpack straps, scratching the furniture and clawing the children. Paul grumbled quietly, but sometimes he egged her on under his breath, hoping I would soon tire of her behavior and find her another home.

Meanwhile, Katzie was still outside, spending most of her time in the pine tree or on the porch roof. Instead of nibbling whenever she was hungry, she ventured to her food dish only when Hansie was penned up, early in the morning and late at night. If Hansie had eaten all her food and no one remembered to replace it, she went hungry.

I was feeling worse and worse about this but didn't know what to do. The final stroke came one evening when I went out late to feed her and saw that she had already been there and left. A line of timid, disappointed, wet pawprints led across the porch to her cat dish and back to the steps.

The next morning, she was gone.

Tortured by regrets, I felt that we had betrayed her trust and she was out there starving in the rain. Paul said cynically that I must be desperate for something to feel guilty about if I felt this bad about a cat.

Even though Paul thought one house cat was far too many, I announced that if Katzie ever showed up again she was going to stay indoors until we could train Hansie to stop chasing her.

Paul was sure she was fine. "She came of her own free will, didn't she? And now she's decided to move on. It has nothing to do with you. She can take care of herself."

I disagreed. She was out there hunting in vain for mice in a soggy ryegrass field, and it was all my fault.

The children and I prayed for Katzie, acknowledging that in the grand scheme of things this cat was not like children dying of malaria and starvation around the world, but still, she was our cat and we were worried. Paul did not join in our prayers but neither, to my knowledge, did he pray that Katzie would stay away.

Then one day when I had despaired of ever seeing her again, Paul called me from his truck. "I'm on my way to Kropf Feed," he said, "and I just thought you might like to know that Katzie is beside the road between us and Coffeys."

"Alive?" I shrieked.

"Alive and licking herself." I could tell he was grinning.

Inside his stern exterior, that man is a softie.

I hurried down the road and there she was, sitting on a piece of wood down in the ditch, skinny and wet but still dignified and beautiful.

Both cats live in the laundry room now but pop into the house whenever the door is open. We take Hansie to dog school every Thursday, where we hope to teach him to respect cats.

Love, as I said, is hard to define, harder still to practice in daily reality. While the red teddy bears sparkle at Big Lots and *National Geographic* analyzes, three couples we know parted ways in the past few weeks.

There is, however, a love that lasts: the kind that puts others' interests and needs ahead of its own preferences.

Downstairs the Queen is Knitting

And this is what it looks like: a tall blond man talking about sermons and orchard grass while absently stroking a fluffy, contented kitten on his lap.

The Rich Recipe of Friendship

My sister-in-law, Bonnie, who is famous for many things but especially her baking, tried out a new cheesecake recipe on us: a rapturous mocha concoction, heavy and brown.

"I'm afraid it's a bit strong on the coffee," she worried. The rest of us thought it was perfect, indulging in a narrow slice to fortify us for shopping, another for walking on the beach, and yet another for a late-night Dutch Blitz game around the table.

Like eggs and cream cheese in cheesecake, the weekend had the basic ingredients that every coast trip ought to have—good food, walks on the beach, shopping and falling asleep to the sound of waves rolling in. But the mocha twist in those few days was this: Instead of a normal family getaway with a van full of sandy shoes and inside-out sweatshirts, this was a dozen Mennonite moms and grandmas luxuriating in a rare break from responsibilities and expectations.

By day, we slept late, shopped at the outlet malls in Lincoln City, and sank into deep leather couches for times of worship and discussion. Outside the sun shone through the wall of windows and the spray blew off the rolling waves in a majestic production that seemed to be specifically for our enjoyment. At night we put on our pajamas and let our hair down, both literally and figuratively. We nibbled on fresh fruit, drank hot chocolate, and broke off just-one-more bites of chocolate-peanut bars. We talked for hours of trivial things—the pros and cons of Curves, the kinds of books our husbands like to read. We also covered many mysterious subjects that women discuss among themselves but never divulge to anyone, especially not their children, who can never quite comprehend that their colorless, one-dimensional mothers have a life and history beyond the four walls of their home.

But mostly, we women laughed—the refreshing, contagious kind of laughter that bubbled up from the depths and rang off the walls, washing over us in a healing wave that left us exhausted yet refreshed, with tears on our cheeks. Ours was a warm and easy laughter, not the shrieks of girls at a slumber party or the brittle laugh of those hardened by life. It was the laughter of traditional, industrious women who grab at a chance to let off steam as eagerly as old-time farmers savored a glass of lemonade in the shade on a hot day.

Curled up in a chair at the end of the table and wiping tears with my flannel-pajama sleeves, I marveled, as I do every year, at how fortunate I was to have these women as friends. They vary as much as the food they brought with them and spread across the counter—grapes, layered chip-dip, bars, and mocha cheesecake. Talkative, quiet, solid, daring, organized, scatterbrained, young, old, and in-between, they all bring something nourishing to my life. Some have mentored me, most have taught me something, all have blessed me.

Rachel shepherded me through our adoption after adopting two daughters of her own.

Bonnie gives me menu ideas when I have no idea what to cook for a family reunion. I know I can call her in a crisis, especially when I find a mouse in my kitchen and need sympathy.

Arlene, like me, is a news junkie, eager to discuss Darfur or trapped coal miners. And, plagued with the same sensitivities as I am, she commiserates when I take a chance remark too personally.

Sharon is determined to pull me into the 21st century. "No, no, no! That's way too old-lady-ish!" she hisses in my ear as I finger a prim, teal, woven-polyester skirt at a Koret store. She wants to sign me up at Curves. It would do me a world of good, she insists, refusing to take no for an answer.

I also have many friends who did not attend our retreat. Rita, for instance, is the one I call when I need someone to pray for me. Judy and I have a habit of what we call, irreverently, "throwing up in each other's laps": in other words, giving much-too-detailed answers when one of us asks, "How are you really doing?" Anita refreshes my soul with elegant servings of tea. Geneva calls me and somehow puts all my problems back in the right perspective.

Back when I was young and choosy, I wanted friends who could join me in what I called "deep discussions," in which we pondered theology, philosophy, and the meaning of life and love. This changed when I had small children and I bonded with other young mothers, connecting instantly with any woman who had a baby on her hip.

Living on a First Nations reserve in Canada and desperate to converse in English, I bonded best with anyone who spoke my language. Thus, I developed friendships with women I would never have gotten to know in a normal setting—teenage Ojibway girls, wild-living nurses, and Shannon, the policeman's wife, who was 10 years younger than me.

Today, it seems that I can find something in common with almost anyone. No one person is all things to me, but each one contributes something unique—advice, mentoring, information, empathy, and support. But most of all, at this stage of my life, I appreciate humor. Through the stresses of parenting, the demands of church work, and the realities of life past 40, laughing with my friends has been a healing thread that keeps me connected to sanity and wholeness.

Sharon and Rachel, for example, think it's their duty to keep me humble. After a Sunday morning church service, when I am trying hard to have a proper-minister's-wife conversation with someone, they stand 10 feet away and whisper to each other, glancing my way like conspirators, and hissing my name just loudly enough for me to hear. It destroys all my concentration and most of my dignity, which is exactly what they want. And we laugh.

Then there is Pauline, whose blunt and precise comments on the world in general and husbands in particular keep me in stitches. And Aunt Susie, who has kept her sense of humor through surgeries on both wrists and knees. Chuckling through her pain, she inspires me.

Susie inspired me again that night at the coast, joining in the fun at an hour when most women her age would have been in bed. Back home, the rest of us also would have been decorously asleep. Instead, on this once-a-year vacation, we lounged around the table, a dozen women swept up in stories and laughter until two in the morning. The low roar of waves in the background contrasted with our voices ringing off the high ceiling and the dark wall of windows. As the night wore on, we talked and teased and giggled, we nibbled on chips and mocha cheesecake, and most of all we savored each bite of the rich concoction of friendship.

Wealth Isn't About the Crayons

$\mathcal{E}$ ven now, I am not quite sure why I bought it. I was at Costco a few weeks ago, scanning the office supplies, and there it was, a thick box of 64 Crayola crayons, with the familiar green and yellow lines slanting down the front.

Perhaps I was simply falling for a clever marketing ploy, but those crayons called to me from 35 years ago, when to own such a box would have meant that God was smiling on me, life was saying "Yes!" and all the doors were opening at last.

So I bought it, and it sits on my desk. The top bends back to reveal tiers of pointed crayons in four neat sections. Wild strawberry, turquoise blue, cerulean, chestnut, and carnation pink. I check and yes, they still make crayons in both green-yellow and yellow-green. It even has that cool little sharpener tucked in the back to keep the crayons perpetually new.

I never had a box of 64 crayons when I was a child. Twelve or 24, maybe, but never a glorious box of 64 like Rachel and Lydia, the two whiny sisters at our little Amish school who did their best to make life miserable for my sister and me. Rachel and Lydia formed "secret" clubs that we were not allowed to join. They hid straight pins in the restroom towels and waited for us to poke our hands. Worse, Rachel and Lydia were rich. They actually got new shoes in the middle of the school year. I, on the other hand, wore holes in my shoes and socks until I sometimes went to school with my big toes exposed. They had pretty notebooks and freely scribbled on a paper, tore it out, and then threw it away—an unthinkable waste.

And they had those big boxes of crayons, a luxury that explained their mysterious power over us, their ability to make us do whatever they wanted even though we resented and even hated them—though we would never have admitted it.

While the Amish are applauded for their sense of community, in some ways they are fiercely independent. To be known as a "poor manager" or to be unable to take care of your family is considered shameful and embarrassing. So my dad, undeniably a "poor manager," taught school for a tiny salary and tried to farm in his spare time, and we were quietly poor. More a scholar than a farmer, Dad bought old, cheap machinery that he didn't know how to fix and farmed with noble but pathetically outdated methods.

Poverty defined our status in the community, our value, and our outlook on life. A black cloud called "The Debt" hung over us, bringing a vague fear of disaster and making us feel that no opportunity would ever knock at our door. Mom filled us up with rice and gravy, vegetables from the garden, chickens that we raised and butchered, and home-made bread. I wore hand-me-down clothes and never had a new coat from a store until I was 19 and on my own.

Much later, I came to realize that poverty and wealth have as much to do with attitudes, comparisons, skills, resources, and a sense of control over one's life as they do with actual dollars or an arbitrary federal poverty level. "Not having money," my brother, Fred, tells me, "is a symptom of being poor. To be poor is to be caught in a cycle of futility, like

going the wrong way on the moving walkway at the airport. Everything works against you, interest on loans piles
up, you always choose the wrong things to invest in. To not
be poor is to go with the walkway. Even if you sit on your
suitcase, you're still moving forward."

To Dad's dismay, my sister and I fantasized about marrying rich men, such as Prince Charles. I did not marry a rich
man, and Paul and I refer to the first 13 years of our marriage as our "Poor Days." But it was a much different sort
of poverty than I had known as a child. Paul had a head
for business, and his clearly defined budget of our meager
monthly income gave me security and a sense of control.
Life could say "yes" even if we were poor, he insisted. When
I needed a serger sewing machine, he figured out how to
save a little bit each month until we could afford it.

When we lived in Canada on a voluntary-worker stipend,
we ate moose meat and rice rather than convenience foods
or fresh fruit, and celebrated the children's birthdays with
homemade cake and huge soap bubbles made with bent
hangers. When Matt was in the bandage-every-bump stage,
his only gift for his fifth birthday was a box of Band-Aids. I
still think he had more fun taping Band-Aids all over himself than he would have had with a $30 remote-control car.
We could never buy much, but with our housing provided
and with Canada's national health plan, we were spared a
sense of impending disaster.

The hardest of our poor days was when we came back
to the United States after eight years in Canada. Instead of
living among equally poor missionaries or the Ojibway, we
were surrounded by an intimidatingly high standard of living. Our children were invited to birthday parties and we
couldn't afford gifts. A church-dinner organizer would hand

me a dessert recipe and ask me to make and bring it. Rather than admit I couldn't afford it, I blew the grocery budget on Cool Whip, Oreos, and fudge sauce.

One of the few things I miss about those days is the thrill of finding a great bargain, but mostly, I am not nostalgic about poverty. Grocery shopping was an agony of decisions, coupons, and calculations. Twice, medical emergencies swallowed all of our savings.

Sometimes, however, I talk to struggling single mothers and realize how wealthy I was in other ways. Thanks to my mom, I had the skills to use cloth diapers, grow and freeze vegetables, and make clothes and food virtually from nothing. Thanks to my constantly employed husband, I had the time.

Our fortunes began to change when we bought a grass seed warehouse business from Paul's dad. Today, if I need to, I can walk into PayLess Shoe Source and buy new shoes for the children. However, since habits from poor days die hard, I bought all their school shoes secondhand this year. Since we remember what it was like, we try to share with others in need.

In spite of our struggles, we have one shining success from our poor days: Our children say they didn't feel poor. When they reminisce about those years, it is not about deprivation and garage-sale gifts but about going on walks, playing by the lake in Canada, and hunting for tadpoles in ditches here in Oregon. Life, they say, felt full of opportunity.

There is one exception to this: Emily, 16, says she will someday bring up in therapy how badly she wanted an American Girl doll and we never bought her one. I imagine her therapist will tell her that now that she is successful and wealthy, she should simply go buy one to heal the wounds of the past.

And Emily will find that it wasn't about dolls at all, just as I found out it wasn't about having 64 crayons. It's about accepting what happened to you, being grateful for the skills and lessons you would not have learned otherwise, and sharing with others. Mostly, it's about forgiving yourself for ever letting Rachel, Lydia, and a box of crayons determine who you were and what you were worth.

About the Author

orcas Smucker, a mother of six and a Mennonite minister's wife, lives in a 98-year-old farmhouse near Harrisburg, Oregon. In addition to her normal responsibilities of pulling splinters, settling arguments, and mopping floors, she writes a column, "Letter from Harrisburg" for the Eugene, Oregon, *Register-Guard*. She also speaks to various groups, which she enjoys because everyone listens and no one interrupts.

Her interests and hobbies include reading, crafts, sewing, travel, and exploring the Internet. She is the author of *Upstairs the Peasants are Revolting* and *Ordinary Days*, also published by Good Books.

If you would like Dorcas Smucker to speak to your group . . .

Dorcas Smucker speaks to groups from time to time as her schedule permits. If you would like to invite her, simply write to her at dorcassmucker@gmail.com.

Here's what some have said...

"We had people coming into the Library asking when she will speak again; her book flies off the shelves. She has been singled out as one of the favorite authors we have had. Her humor and insight speak to all faiths, nationalities, and sexes."

—*Friends of the Junction City Library*

"Dorcas was excellent and talked to a full house. The evaluations of her presentation, from those who attended, were A+."

—*Program Planner for OASIS, a senior-learning organization*

"Dorcas speaks from her heart in a gentle, honest way that resonates with her listeners. She speaks much like she writes."

—*Oregon Christian Writers Program Coordinator*

"I invited Dorcas to speak to my third-grade class on writing. Her presentation was outstanding! She had 60 third-grade students enthralled for over 30 minutes. She had an instant rapport with the group, and we will definitely invite her back."

—*Teacher at Spring Creek Elementary School*

Also by Dorcas Smucker

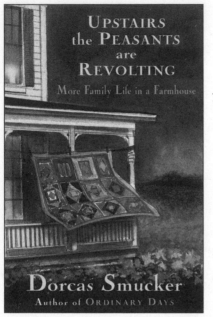

Upstairs the Peasants are Revolting
More Family Life in a Farmhouse
168 pages • $9.95, paperback
ISBN: 978-1-56148-600-7

Ordinary Days
Family Life in a Farmhouse
155 pages • $9.95, paperback
ISBN: 978-1-56148-522-2

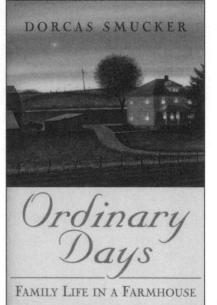